JUST KEEPIN'
IT REAL, LADIES

-A MALE PERSPECTIVE ON RELATIONSHIPS-

BACK TO BASICS

BY JAMAL WATTERS

Edited By Amanda Brown

-Photography by Desmond Rogers-

Men of Images Publishing

This book is dedicated to my beautiful daughter, Kayla Watters. I want you to know that your mother and I thank God every day for blessing us with such an incredibly special gift. I encourage you to ALWAYS love yourself and let this be your guiding light in love and life. With this book, I hope to make the world a better place for you tomorrow than it is today. Hugs and kisses!

Table of Contents

-BONUS CHAPTERS-

Acknowledgments

I would first of all like to thank God because without him this book would not be possible. Mom and Pop: I would like to thank my mother, Doris Stewart, for giving birth to me, raising me to be the man that I am, and instilling in me love and respect for women. I love you, Mom, for always showing me unconditional love and support! I would like to thank my father. Although there was more distance between us geographically than I would have liked growing up, I appreciate you always making your presence felt and providing a listening ear when I needed it...it meant a lot. Wife and Daughter: I would like to thank my wife, Letitia Watters, for her amazing love, understanding, and always trusting and believing in me even when I've doubted myself at times. I love you, babe! I would like to thank my daughter, Kayla Watters, because you are my primary motivation and inspiration for writing this book. I wanted to give you something in your daddy's words, if ever we're apart, that will help you make the right choices when it comes to men. Hopefully you will someday find happiness with a man who will treat you with all the love you deserve. Daddy loves you more than anything! Sis: I thank you for being the consummate big sis, always showing me love and support, and always having my back! In-laws: Thank you mother-in-law, Barbara Flaherty, and sister-in-law, Robin Flaherty, for showing me love, support and encouragement always...much love and appreciation! I also want to thank my two brothers-in-law, Jerry Flaherty and Michael Flaherty for being awesome brothers. My dawgs: Thank you Mark Collins (AKA Mark Cee), William Uschold (AKA Will-U) Steve Parham (AKA Money Mac and Dinero), Jeff

Stewart, Cornell Slaton (AKA Corn Soul), Melvin Lawrence, and Curtis Lee Holmes for being my dawgs and my true brothers from another mother. Much Love! I want to give a special acknowledgment to my dawg Mark Collins for being the co-creator of Men of Images that ultimately led to me writing this book. And the wives of my dawgs, Rickesha Collins, Erica Uschold, and Tiffany Parham: Thank you, ladies, for always exemplifying class and grace. Extended family: Thanks to my aunts (Elaine Stewart, Barbara Fonteno, Stephanie Watters, Evon Cage, Joyce Brooks-RIP, and Lazetta Stewart-RIP) for being strong, influential women in my life. Also thanks to my uncles (Albert Stewart, James Stewart, and Lawrence Fonteno) for being positive male figures in my life and demonstrating that there are "real" men who can commit. Big ups to all my cousins, too many to name everyone, but I love you all! Special shout out to my nephews, Josh and Jeremiah Widemon and Xavier Harris, and godsons Marque Collins and Mylo Uschold. Alameda County: A special thanks to my Alameda County family, particularly all the women I have ever known at the County. Thanks for all the love, encouragement, support, and sharing your personal relationship stories with me. You all hold a special place in my heart! Lastly, I want to thank my 49th street family, who played an important role in influencing and shaping the man I have become. You too will always hold a special place in my heart.

Anyone I may have missed-THANK YOU!

About the Author

Jamal Watters was born and raised in Oakland, CA. He was raised by his mother, a single parent, who he credits for all of his early teachings about love, respect, and appreciation for women. Jamal first became interested in relationships through watching his mother struggle as a single parent. He could not help but imagine what life would've been like for his mother if she had a loving and devoted husband by her side to help raise him and his sister. He realized at a very early age that relationships are a central part of who we are, and what we observe and experience from early on in life plays a very important role in how we deal with relationships as we grow older. That's why Jamal strongly believes healthy relationships equal healthy families.

As a youth growing up in Oakland and being raised by a single parent, Jamal was faced with many challenges. But through the grace of God, his mother's guidance, and his love for football, he was able to overcome these challenges. Although Jamal garnered much attention while playing football, he used this talent as a catalyst to further his education. Jamal earned a Bachelor's degree in Sociology and a Master's in Social Work. He also holds a clinical license to practice therapy, in which he currently counsels couples on relationships. His approach to therapy, no doubt, is Keepin' it Real. Jamal believes that his real and genuine approach to working with people is why he is so effective. He also employs a key principal that he learned from football in counseling couples as well as in his own relationship, which is—when things get too complicated, go back to the basics. Jamal believes we commonly make things much more complicated than they have to be and we forget about doing the little things such as communicating, compromising, not taking each other for granted, dating, working together to achieve common goals, and so forth. Jamal quotes his mother as saying, "The same thing it took to get yo' baby hooked is what it will take to keep them."

Although Jamal is a licensed therapist, he contributes most of his insight into relationships to real life experiences. His first teachings were from his mother and later from observing his sister in her relationships. He then expanded his knowledge of relationships through various women he encountered in school, work, and social experiences.

Jamal has been happily married for over seventeen years and has been with his wife for twenty-four years. He believes the longevity he has with his wife has given him invaluable insight. It is because of the insight Jamal has gained from both his personal and professional life that he wanted to fill a need he felt was missing... the male perspective on relationships. Combined with insight from real life experiences, Jamal infuses his background in sociology and psychology to give women real and relatable concepts on relationships. It is Jamal's strong affinity for women that stems from his mother and later his wife and daughter that made him want to write a book he hopes will serve as a useful guide for all women.

Introduction

Just Keepin' It Real, Ladies is a book that delivers real and relatable concepts to women with the purpose of providing insight and understanding into the male mind. By offering a male perspective, my goal is to empower women to make more informed choices when it comes to men. For years, women were only exposed to dealing with men from a woman's perspective by magazines such as *Cosmopolitan, People, Essence* or *Ebony.* And for a long time, the male voice, and perspective, was missing. A big reason for that missing piece was that men traditionally were not accustomed to expressing or communicating their thoughts and feelings. And while men will probably never become the open book that women would like to see, more men nowadays are opening up about relationships and the opposite sex. The male perspective is still sparse, nevertheless. But I credit men for now sharing their perspective on relationships to try to "bridge the gap" of understanding between men and women. I view this bridge as the missing piece of the puzzle.

That said... my goal in offering a male perspective on relationships is not intended to put women down or make excuses for why men do what they do. It's also not meant to pit men against women, like battle of the sexes or love and war. It's about men and women learning how to form healthier, long lasting relationships. The reality is relationships are a two-way street... both men and women have an equal responsibility to make the relationship work. So in my book, I try to keep it real with women on what I have come to learn about relationships through my years of experience and education. Therefore, I have provided some basic concepts that will help women navigate the sometimes murky waters of a male's mind. In other words, this book will help guide women as they try to understanding what makes most men tick.

In this book, women will learn some of the differences between men and women, some essential ingredients that go into developing a healthy relationship with a man, why men do some of the things they do, how to communicate with a man, some things that turn men on and off, and some red flags to look for among other things. With that said... it's important to point out relationships cannot always be viewed as black and white, summed up in *abc* terms, or put into one-two-three steps. All relationships are unique and should be assessed based on the individual qualities and characteristics of the two people who make up the relationship.

CHAPTER 1

Do Men Really Know What Women Want?

Ladies... if you were to ask most men if they know what women want... the response you'd probably get would be a resounding *NO!* Followed by an even louder *HELL NO!* I'm just keepin' it real.

One main reason is that some women are just too damn confusing. That's right. I said it! Trying to figure some women out is harder than trying to figure out Chinese arithmetic. But seriously, ladies, what confuses men sometimes are the mixed messages that leave them scratching their heads like what just happened?

For instance, a mixed message that some women are guilty of is saying you want a man who's not afraid to take charge. But when you meet one, you won't allow him to be a man because you need to be in control. Now I get it... it may not be easy for some of you to give up control because this is what your experience has taught you. Some of you feel that you need to be in control because of past disappointments with men. You are afraid to let down your guard. Others have been faced with the challenge of being single parents, and some have had to take charge in the boardroom.

But with all due respect, ladies, you have to understand that control does not work very well in the bedroom—in a manner of speaking. You cannot do things like emasculate a man and at the same time expect him to exert himself as the man of the household. Nor, ladies, can you take past experiences and apply them to every man you meet.

I'm not saying you have to give up control entirely and rely on a man to run everything because being independent and self-sufficient are great qualities to have. What I am saying is a man wants and needs to feel like he is a part of your world and not like he is on the outside looking in. In other words, you have to let a man be a man and understand that a man likes to feel needed. If you have a "good" man, you should be able to trust that he will know what his responsibilities are as a man, and he will demonstrate this by his actions if you allow him to.

Men Are Not Psychic

Another important reason why most men do not really know what women want is that men are not mind readers. On the real, some women expect men to just know what they are thinking and how they feel. Now I will admit that men could be a little more—okay, a lot more—in tune with the needs, wants, and desires of women, but the reality is men are just not programmed that way.

Sorry, ladies, on behalf of men for our shortcomings in this area. But again, please do not assume that men will know where you are coming from if you don't communicate directly to them your wants, needs, and desires. You have to be CLEAR, DIRECT, and most of all HONEST (especially with yourself) about what you want if you truly expect a man to meet your needs.

For instance, when you meet a man and are looking for more than just a "friend with benefits," you need to be honest and clear about that. Don't lead him to believe that you're okay with just a casual hook up because you don't want to scare him off. This is misleading, especially if you know you want more. If you think a man will change his mind after you've worked your feminine wiles on him, nine times out of ten, he will not. It's best to be straight with him from the start, which will save you from heartache and keep you from wasting your time on a guy that can't really give you what you want.

If a man does not want the same thing you do, at least you were honest about your feelings and there were no hidden agendas or games being played. A man will definitely respect you more for your honesty, and you will know if he is potentially the right person for you. I'm certainly not telling you that you have to pour out all of your thoughts and feelings on the first date, but it is definitely important for a guy to know where you stand sooner than later in terms of your expectations.

Men are also not very good at picking up on subtle cues, hints, signs, and so on. Men like it straight and to the point. As I previously mentioned, ladies, you have to be honest, clear and direct about what you want from a man. I've talked to many women who have reached the "critical" age of thirty, are established in their careers, and are looking to settle down and start a family. These women feel that time is vital, and they certainly don't want to waste a lot of time dealing with the wrong guy while their biological clock is ticking.

But, ladies, telling a man that your best friend just got engaged after two years of dating when you've been seeing your man for five years may not be enough for him to get the message that you want a ring. Buying bridal magazines or watching shows like Platinum weddings in his presence again may not be enough to get him to the altar.

That's why I stress to women the importance of being open, honest and direct about how you feel and what you want. Expressing your wants, needs, and desires should not scare a "real" man off. This will only help him understand you better and vice versa. You should also feel comfortable asking a man deeper, meaningful questions to get to know him better. A "real" man will not see this as an inquisition or interrogation and should appreciate the fact that you are interested in what makes him tick.

Timing and a Little Bit of Honey Can Make a Big Difference

I want to point out two other important reasons why men have a hard time knowing what women want. It is not just what you say or don't say, ladies. It is how and when you choose to tell a man your wants and desires. Again, I'm just keepin' it real.

If you're accustomed to communicating to your man by nagging, screaming, dictating to him, or using a punitive tone like the ever-classic line "We need to talk," this will probably not get you what you want in most cases. Most men will either tune you out or shut down because not just men (people in general) have a hard time responding to this style of negative communication.

It is said that you can catch more flies with honey, so a suggestion would be talking to your man in a calm and respectful manner. You'll definitely increase your chances of being heard. Now of course, this goes both ways and applies to men as well. Healthy relationships are about mutual respect.

Timing is also extremely important when you want to have a deep, meaningful discussion with your man about your relationship. Now I know in some situations, poor timing is unavoidable. But if you just want to hear your man tell you how much he loves you or want to know if he is truly happy in the relationship, it might not be the best time to have this discussion during the fourth quarter of the Super Bowl, at 2 a.m. when he has to get up at 5 a.m. for work, or when he comes home from a very tough day at the office. Com' on, ladies, I'm just saying this is not when a man will be most attentive, and you probably will not get the response that you are looking for.

It is also said that the way to a man's heart is through his stomach. So a suggestion might be to consider having certain meaningful conversations over a nice dinner either prepared by you or your treat. Surprise him, especially if he deserves it. Other suggestions might be to express your needs and desires while going for a walk, or plan a small trip or get away, just the two of you (especially if you have children) where you have each other's undivided attention.

That said—I get it, ladies. It is not always easy to be honest and direct with men about how you feel because of various reasons. Maybe you don't want to come across as desperate, maybe you are afraid of rejection, maybe you don't want to "rock the boat," or maybe you don't want to seem like you're always causing drama. But if you want a man to really know what you want, you have to communicate in a way that men will understand you. At the end of the day, communication is one of the most important elements of any successful relationship.

Recap: Control does not work well in the bedroom, ladies. If you trust your own judgment in picking a good guy who is responsible, then trust that he will make good decisions in your and his best interest. Be clear, honest, and direct with your man about your wants, needs, and desires. And remember, timing and how you communicate with a man are very important.

CHAPTER 2

Why Some Women Can't Find Mr. Right

Women have often asked me the question, "Why can't I find Mr. Right? Does he really exist? And my response is...maybe Mr. Right is right in front of you but you haven't taken the time to notice him, or maybe you can't see him because you are spending too much time on the wrong man and you are missing your opportunity to meet Mr. Right. This is real talk, ladies... before you can begin to know what it is you are looking for in a man you have to really know yourself first. Here's what I mean...

Now I believe many women set themselves up to fail in their pursuit to find Mr. Right because of their unrealistic expectations or overly rigid or too high standards. You know the classic saying, "I want a man who's tall, dark, and handsome." Well, women have taken this to a whole other level and the list has gotten a lot more extensive. For instance, women nowadays want a man to have money, status, power, be 6'2" tall, have good hair with light eyes, be good in bed, have a great body, be romantic, have A-1 credit, and massage their feet when they come home. Daaaamn! What if your feet are crusty with bunions or they look like you've been playing in the sand box? Com' on, ladies, you can't really expect a man to massage those feet! But all jokes aside, I'm not saying you shouldn't have standards, but they should never be so high or rigid that no man could possibly meet them all.

Let's take Chilli from the singing group TLC, for example. A few years back she had a reality show about "What Chilli Wants," and she had a very specific checklist of the type of man she was looking for. The list went something like this: Her man had to believe in God, have a six-pack, be well-endowed, be super fine, couldn't drink, couldn't smoke, and couldn't eat pork to name a few. Wow! What's wrong with a man just having a three-pack?

But on the real, I respect Chilli and women in general who have standards and believe they know what they are looking for in a man. Ladies, you should have some idea of the type of man you are looking for. But I believe before you begin looking for a man, you need to ask yourself, "What do I bring to the table?" and "What are some of my own issues?" Am I too emotionally needy? Do I have control or trust issues? Baby daddy drama? Is my attitude too negative? Am I too high maintenance? Am I too conceited? Or do I listen to my girlfriends too much about my relationship?

Some women walk around with the "Cinderella Syndrome" hoping to be rescued by their prince charming. But he has to have a six-figure salary and be driving a Mercedes. What if he drove a Prius but was a very nice guy and hardworking? Would you automatically shoot him down without getting to know him?

First of all, ladies, you can't expect a man to have everything you want because no one is perfect. Second, you can't expect a man to have everything you want if you are not offering the same thing in return. And I don't just mean physically or financially but mentally and spiritually. These qualities make a woman the "complete package." Now in Chilli's case, she appears to be the complete package and I'm sure she has no problem attracting men. But it begs the question...are her standards realistic and can a man ever truly measure up. Are Chilli's issues just about having standards that are too high, or are there some possible control issues as well? In any case, this may be a big reason why Chilli and other women with overly high or unrealistic standards might have a difficult time finding Mr. Right. I'm just saying...

Ladies, a man may not fit your checklist exactly, but if he's a good person, is hard-working, and respects you, isn't that what's most important? I'm not saying a man should not have certain qualities that are important to you because there might be some definite deal breakers—like someone who lacks ambition, or someone who lies or cheats. I'm just saying don't close the door on a man too soon just because he does not fit everything you want.

The truth is every man is not going to look like Morris Chestnut, Trey Songz, Brad Pitt, or Channing Tatum, or have power like Obama, or be ballin' like Jay Z or have "crazy" money like Warren Buffet or Bill Gates. Not to mention, everything that glitters ain't gold. Think about these possibilities, ladies, when choosing someone based solely or primarily on superficial qualities. You might end up with a guy who is too driven to spend time with you (and I know what spending quality time means to a woman). He could be someone who treats you like a possession, or he could be someone who thinks he is God's gift to women so he can't be completely faithful to you. These are some real possibilities to consider when selecting a man based on the outer person. Shouldn't it be more about the character of man than his physical attributes, wealth, status, or other superficial qualities?

Lowering Your Standards

Now, when it comes to standards, I think the extreme opposite is another common mistake that contributes to some women not being able to find Mr. Right. These women set their standards so low they choose the worst type of guy. Be careful, ladies, with sending this type of mixed signal and be clear about what you want.

I hear women say all the time that they want a man who will respect them, but at the same time, they will choose a bad boy, thug, or rough neck over a good guy. This is a contradiction, ladies, and it sends a very confusing message to men. You can't have it both ways. If a man is conservative, too nice, attentive, or sensitive, he is perceived as being a "square" or "too soft," and because of this, the guy gets dogged out. Then he dogs out the next woman and the cycle continues. If you really want a bad boy, thug, or rough neck, let's be real about it, that's exactly what you are going to get. And you shouldn't be surprised if this type of guy has a hard time staying committed, treats you with very little respect, is possessive, aggressive, or even violent. These are just some possibilities if you chose to lower your standards and deal with a bad boy, thug, or rough neck type of guy.

Don't get me wrong, ladies, having standards that are too high or too low are not the only reasons why women find it difficult to meet Mr. Right, but they are some very common mistakes that women make time and time again...

The bottom line is you should have standards, ladies, but try to be a little flexible if a man does not fit everything you want entirely. The truth is no one is perfect, but there may be someone out there perfect for you if you just open yourself up to him without all the conditions and recognize his inner qualities. Also take the time to know yourself before you try to find a man because you may be surprised to learn that your own issues may be the reason you have not found Mr. Right.

Recap: Check your own issues, ladies, before you go looking for a man. KNOW your deal breakers and don't compromise this, everything else is negotiable. Be consistent and clear about what you want, and don't send mixed signals. It's also important to have standards, but make sure they're realistic and reasonable. Remember... no one is perfect.

CHAPTER 3

Why Do Men Cheat?

Wow, the infamous question—why do men cheat?

I can't count how many times women have asked me this question.

My question to you, ladies, is—can you handle the truth?

First, some might say the simple or short answer to why men cheat is that women allow men to cheat. But in my opinion, that is way too easy a response to a not-so-easy question and it puts the blame on women. It also implies that a woman can control a man's actions. Now I do believe once a man has cheated, if there are no real consequences to his actions, a woman is sending the message that she is willing to accept this behavior or mistreatment. But again the idea of women allowing men to cheat is oversimplifying the act of cheating or, more specifically, why men cheat. The fact of the matter is, it boils down to an individual choice and men have to take responsibility for their actions just as women do.

Breaking It Down—Why Men Cheat...

That said... just keeping it one hundred, ladies, the reality is there is no simple answer or single reason why a man cheats. The fact is, the reason a man cheats may be different for different men depending on the situation. Men also cheat for different reasons than women. Yeah I said it, women cheat too! Men are not cheating all by themselves. It takes two to tango

But in a woman's case, I have found that it is not so easy for a woman to cheat on her man because it's hard for her to separate the physical nature of a sexual relationship from her emotions. I believe if a woman is TRULY in love with a man and cheats, you can bet it took a lot to drive her to this point. In other words, a woman has to be seriously disrespected, mistreated, neglected or emotionally abused for her to cheat on her man (BUT NOT ALWAYS). I used the term seriously because it is not just one screw up by a man that leads a woman to cheat. Usually several indiscretions or acts of being mistreated tear a woman down and makes her more inclined to seek attention from another man.

But getting back to the question of why men cheat, there are a myriad of different reasons why men cheat. Of course, men will usually only admit these reasons to their homeboys because men don't like to admit JACK you-know-what, even if caught in the act.

Here is a list of some common reasons why men have admitted they cheat...

- I cheated because I was tired of the drama at home.
- We don't talk like we used to.

- She does sexual things that you won't do.
- I'm not getting any at home.
- Or, like Jamie Foxx said, "Blame it on the alcohol."
- Or just plain and simple—she looked good and had a stripper body.

These may sound like excuses, but not all of the reasons I mentioned are unjustified, for lack of a better word, whether you want to hear it or not. One of the quickest way to chase a man away and into the bed of another woman is drama at home or his perception of there being drama. I'm not condoning or excusing men by ANY means for cheating ... I'm just keepin' it real as to why men generally speaking do cheat.

However, some reasons are not so justified and one of the most common reasons men cheat as mentioned is simply they just liked the other woman physically. But I want to stress to you, ladies, that if a man cheats for this reason, it is not because of something you did or didn't do. Nor is it whether a man likes the other woman more or loves you any less. Men are visual in that they are drawn to what they see and usually have sex on the brain most of the time. So if another woman looks good, has a nice body, and has a certain sexual allure, this can sometimes be enough to make men think about wanting to "hit it," even if they do not always act on it. Men are very good at detaching the physical aspect of a sexual relationship from their emotions. Sex for them can be just purely physical.

Another major reason men have a harder time controlling their sexual impulses and are more prone to cheat than woman is because of the way men are generally socialized and conditioned. Don't get me wrong, both men and women have a natural primal instinct to have their sexual needs met.

However, the way men approach sexual relationships is very different than women.

The reason is that men are largely socialized to view women as sex objects by different male figures in their lives, friends, television, magazines and the media. You see it all the time with athletes like Mike Tyson, Kobe Bryant and Tiger Woods to name a few, and politicians such as Clinton and Arnold Schwarzenegger, even ministers, as well as in countless music videos. Women also exploit themselves by using their looks and bodies as their main asset and again this reinforces the idea of viewing women as sex objects.

The concept of men viewing women as sex objects and men pursuing women goes back a long time. Even in the early times of cave men and women, a man would see a woman he wants, club her over the head, and carry her back to his cave. Essentially, men have been taught to chase women, conquer them, and get as many notches on their belt as they can. The message is strong that a man is not a "real" man unless he has slept with many women. The more women a man sleeps with, the more respect he gets from other males. This message is programmed in a male's mind from a very early age, and as he grows, it continues to be reinforced. For some men it becomes difficult to change this way of thinking.

That said... there are many reasons men cheat, as mentioned. Possibly they're trying to fill a void that's not being met at home, escape the drama of home, are the product of how they were socialized, or just for plain old sexual reasons...

But you can exhale now, ladies, because not all men are "dogs" and more importantly NOT ALL MEN CHEAT!

Some possible signs of a CHEATER:

- Suddenly becoming distant. But first look at any recent events that may otherwise explain this behavior such as significant life stressors (i.e., pressures at work, loss of a job, death in the family, etc.).
- Breaking dates or not showing up on time because someone else may be consuming his time.
- More annoyed or irritated with basic conversation, especially about your relationship.
- Noticeable changes in behavior (paying special attention to appearance, staying later at work when it's not that type of job, edgy or moody with simple affection, stories are not consistent or make sense, always claiming to be out with the fellas).
- Looking for justification to ease guilt by projecting problems in the relationship on you and creating reasons to argue and fight so that he can leave the house.
- Being evasive.
- Being secretive.
- Your GUT or INSTINCT is telling you something is wrong.

Recap: There are many reasons that men cheat, just as some women cheat. But cheating is still an individual choice at the end of the day and each individual has to take responsibility for their own actions.

And once again, ladies... NOT ALL MEN CHEAT.

CHAPTER 4

Why Do Men Cheat? Part 2...Should I Stay or Should I Go?

Prelude to Part 2...

In my chapter "Why Do Men Cheat," I offered women some insight on the various reasons why men cheat. Based on some of the women's responses to that chapter, it seems clear that some women still feel, regardless of the reasons, men are just making excuses to justify their actions. Women believe that men should be more honest, able to communicate better, not give into temptation, and work out whatever drama there might be at home, just like women are able to do.

Well first, this goes both ways, ladies, because as I said before men are not cheating alone... let's keep it real. That said, I hear you and agree that men could do better job addressing whatever issues there are in the relationship before they decide to cheat. But as nice as that sounds, the point is men and women are different in how they think and in the way they are socialized to behave.

Now I'm not suggesting that men are incapable of being in a committed relationship or being honest in a relationship, I'm just saying that men see and approach relationships differently than women based on how they are socialized. Women are taught to express their feelings through communication, men are taught not to talk about their feelings or show their true emotions (remember, ladies... it is said that a man is not supposed to cry). Women are taught that one day they will meet their "prince charming," fall in love, and live happily ever after in a monogamous relationship, whereas men are taught to enjoy a plethora of women by sowing their wild oats. Women also mature faster than men developmentally, while men take longer to mature and figure out who they are and what they want in life, generally speaking.

These are real considerations, ladies, not just excuses. Sure some men, despite how they are generally socialized, are fortunate to have positive role models to teach and instill in them trust, honesty, commitment, and respect for women as well as how to communicate within a relationship. So yes, I do think there are men who don't cheat, but in my opinion, these men have become more the exception than the rule. Otherwise there wouldn't be this resounding question "WHY DO MEN CHEAT." The same can be said for women who learn to think and act like men when it comes to the issue of cheating. Again I believe these women are also exceptions to the rule (although I will say the gap between men and women who cheat nowadays is narrowing). But I think we all can agree that whatever the reason a person cheats, man or woman, it is wrong and everyone has to be accountable for the choices they make.

On to Part 2...

Now as far as men who cheat or have cheated, the topic begs the question—should I stay or should I go? This is a question many women have asked themselves after they have been cheated on...

Ladies, I can't tell you that if you do all the right things your man won't cheat on you. The fact is there are many reasons men cheat, and for some men, cheating is not so much about you as it is about the man himself. You can't stop a man from cheating if he's that type of guy. He's going to cheat anyway. Again, it basically comes down to an individual choice and the man has to be accountable for his own actions.

But if you have been cheated on, the decision to stay or go is definitely a personal choice. Understandably, it is not always an easy choice to make because things are not always black and white especially if you really love that person. On the other hand, for some women, it may be a "deal breaker" and for them it's easier to move on. I know some of your girlfriends might have you believe that it is easy to deal with the issue of cheating by saying, "Girrrl... you need to leave him because all men are dogs."

The reality is love hurts and it is complicated. Also, you might want to ask yourself whether they are telling you this because they genuinely care about you, or does misery love company? Possibly they are interested in your man themselves. Think about it!

Well, ladies... let me keep it real with you as always and give you some things to consider if your man cheats on you. First, I want to say that it is a natural reaction for you to be extremely upset, hurt, disappointed, angry, and you might even want to kill him and the other woman. But don't do it, ladies! These are all normal emotions that go along with a man betraying your trust. Now as I said, the issue of cheating is not always simple or black and white. Every situation is different and you have to assess it differently. You cannot generalize or relate it to what happened to your friend, cousin, or your friend's cousin's uncle's baby momma.

Second, after the initial shock and blow up, and of course there might be some cussing, screaming, and burning of his clothes (yeah I've seen the movie *Waiting to Exhale*), you should look at the situation closely and carefully. You need to ask yourself if this is the first time he's cheated on you or has it been many times? I believe the two are very different, although cheating is devastating whether it is one time or many times.

If it is the first time, you need to look at the overall situation and ask yourself whether you believe in your heart of hearts that your man TRULY loves you despite him cheating. If you don't believe this or you've had doubts for some time, you may want to consider other options.

If you genuinely believe that your man loves you, you want to look at whether he is a good man overall. Then you want to consider how much time you have invested together. This is important because if you just met the guy or you've only known him a short time, his commitment to you may be highly suspect anyway. If you have time invested and your man cheats, you really should try to communicate with him and LISTEN to why he says he cheated. If you don't give him the opportunity to speak or listen to him, he will either become afraid to open up to you about his real feelings or totally shut down. He may feel as though what is the point.

It is good to give him a chance to explain no matter how upset you are or whether you feel his reasons are not sufficient or justified. I'm not telling you to believe everything he tells you because you definitely have to filter out the Bull S#@t from the truth. But his reasoning is what he believes, and you should take note of these reasons especially if he makes a valid point such as you stopped having sex with him or communicating with him. Or if he says you are constantly nagging or criticizing him or you stopped doing things to be sexy or desirable like you did in the beginning.

You may not agree that any reason he gives is good enough, but you can't discount that these things are clear signs that there is a breakdown in the relationship. If not addressed, these issues can lead to a man's infidelity or a woman's for that matter. Sure it's not always about you, but in some cases it is and it is important to be aware of this.

Just being real, ladies, if you see yourself doing any of the things I mentioned, it should not come as a total surprise that your man stepped out on you. Because the truth is, plenty of women (AKA The Clean-Up Woman!) are looking for a man themselves and will gladly step in and do the things that you won't do or stopped doing to maintain the relationship. However, I do believe that if you have been cheated on, you can rebuild your relationship if you truly want to. But it will take time, forgiveness, and plenty of reassurance and proving on HIS part that he will never cheat again (BY HIS ACTIONS, not just in words).

That said, not all men who cheat have justifiable reasons, but it is up to you to decide what is acceptable, or not, and what is worth fighting for. I think if both of you are willing to work it out and your man is truly remorseful, you can start to rebuild the trust and the relationship. And, ladies, this is VERY IMPORTANT, if you say you forgive your man, please do not continue to hold this over his head or throw it in his face every time you have an argument. Let the past be the past.

Don't say you trust him if you know deep down you don't. And you believe every time he goes to the store or hangs out with the guys, he is out cheating. You've got to stay out of his pockets, stop checking his emails, cell phone, Facebook page, underwear (yeah I said underwear), and questioning his every move unless he proves otherwise. If this is the case, you may want to seriously consider letting him go because this will only push him further away and into the next woman's arms. But more importantly, it will ultimately drive you crazy. You have to be real with him and most of all yourself.

On the other hand, if you are hooked up with a habitual, chronic, or serial cheater, you need to figure out whether he is the fool or you are the fool for staying with him. I'm sorry, ladies, com' on. I don't care how much you think you love a man, you've got to love yourself more. And let's be honest, some of you will meet a serial cheater with flirtatious tendencies, know of his questionable past when it comes to cheating, and for some reason still choose to get involved with him.

If you continue to ignore the obvious red flags or lower your standards, you're opening yourself up to nothing but heartache. And if you have been cheated on, you have to set firm limits and make it perfectly clear what you expect (a ZERO cheating policy from here on out and STICK TO IT). Otherwise, you are sending the message to him that it's okay to cheat because there are no real consequences to his actions. You are essentially conditioning him to think and believe that he can get away with cheating any time he wants and you will take him back. If you love and respect yourself, a real man will love and respect you and do his best to be a good man. If a man does not respect you, it should be pretty obvious that he is not the one for you and you need to let him know to keep it moving.

Recap: Making the decision to stay or go if you've been cheated on is not always an easy choice, but it is YOUR choice to make. After the initial feelings of shock, anger, and disappointment, it's good to hear the person out and weigh all the facts before you decide whether you want to stay with the person or not. Regardless of your decision, you want to make sure it is right for you. And very important, if you decide to forgive the person who cheated, make sure you REALLY mean it. It doesn't mean you have to forget, but you can learn to trust again.

CHAPTER 5

Why Men Find It Hard to Commit

Ladies... if you're dealing with a man who has commitment issues, I will give you some general concepts that I hope will help you understand him (and men in general) better. But before you apply these concepts to any man, you need to first rule out other possible causes that might attribute to a man's commitment issues, such as dealing with trust issues from a previous relationship or is it related to his childhood experience. If either is the case, I recommend you both seek professional guidance because these types of commitment issues are harder to get resolved, if ever. I'm just keepin' real. You can find yourself wasting a lot of time on a man who is incapable of committing to you or anyone else. That said, I'm sure most men have struggled with the decision to commit at one time or another. Here's why...

The truth is a lot of men are terrified when they hear the word **commit** or suspect that the relationship is headed in that direction. What can I say, ladies... most men have a commitment phobia. One primary reason most men fear commitment is that they are afraid of picking the wrong woman to settle down with. But contrary to popular belief, a man is more inclined to settle down if he feels the woman he is with is the right one. And while a woman might think she is the right one, the question is does the guy feel she is the right one for him? The truth is, ladies, you can have a lot of amazing qualities, but there may be something about you that is causing the man you're with to take it slow or not want to commit at all. You shouldn't try to force what might not be right for you either.

Another reason men fear commitment is that they are socialized to believe that it is natural to have a plethora, a stable, a harem, or whatever term is used to describe a man who wants to have a relationship (usually of a sexual nature) with many women at one time. This is a concept that is embedded in a male's psyche from a very early age. It starts with the message, "Ooooh... he's so cute... he's going to be a ladies' man when he grows up and have all the women chasing him." As he grows, this message becomes further entrenched in his mind through different media streams and social interactions like television, magazines, and male peer relations. Essentially, males are taught to be "players," which by definition, according to the urban dictionary and popularized by the hip hop culture, is someone who is very skilled at manipulating ("playing") others and especially at seducing many women by pretending to care about them, when in reality they are only interested in sex.

I will admit this sounds bad from a male's standpoint, but not all men adopt or subscribe to this type of behavior or way of thinking as they grow older. However, the message to avoid commitment by any means is still very strong. Women also play a key role in adding to this message by excusing a man's infidelity and not offering up any real consequences to his actions. Some women even live with their man and have children without demanding or requiring a real commitment from him. The saying is "why buy the cow if you can get the milk for free." In other words, the man has all the benefits of having a wife so there is no real incentive for him to fully invest or commit to the woman he is with. This is real talk!

To further add to the message of men wanting to have relationships with multiple women at a given time, it seems that far more women are out pacing men when it comes to education, finances, and stability. When you find a man who has all of these qualities to offer, he is viewed as a hot commodity. Because of this, the man believes that he can have his pick of any woman he wants (i.e., like a kid in a candy store) and is less likely to want to commit to just one woman. Let's be real about it, ladies, would you?

Another important point that I want to make about males being socialized in avoiding commitment is that it is more socially acceptable for men to take their time when it comes to relationships and explore or sow their wild oats before settling down. Conversely, women are not socialized that way. With women, the message traditionally has been to find a man and settle down (although this has changed some in recent times). It's not considered socially acceptable for women to be with this guy, that guy, and the other guy. It's not seen as being very "lady like." I'm not saying I agree with this double standard, but I'm just pointing out a fundamental difference in how men and women are socialized. Because women are more pressured to pick a guy and settle down with him, I believe a woman is more inclined to make a situation work by working with a guy even if he is not necessarily the most ideal guy for her.

Men also avoid commitment to escape the idea of giving up their freedom and autonomy. A lot of men feel they will no longer be free to hang out with the guys or just act immature or silly for no good reason. They feel this also means they have to do things like give up video games because this is perceived as acting "childlike," adhere to a curfew, trade in the sports car for a Volvo, and only do the things that are considered to be "responsible." In effect, this means he has to grow up, and some men are simply afraid to accept this fact. This really boils down to where the guy might be in his level of maturity, which equates to his readiness to settle down.

A final point I want to make concerning the reason men find it hard to commit is that most men are socialized to believe that to be a "real" man you have to be the bread winner. Regardless of how much money a woman makes, a man feels ultimately responsible to take care of his household. This means keeping a roof over his family's head, food on the table, clothes on their backs, paying the bills, and being successful in his career. A man will feel less than a man (even though most men have a hard time admitting this fact because of pride) and find it hard to commit if he has not achieved certain success in his life. You have to understand, ladies, that men have a tough time rationalizing when you say, "Babe, we're in this together and I will do my part." Although this sounds good in theory and may be true, men still feel the pressure to provide for the family ultimately.

Financial security is EXTREMELY important to a male's manhood in terms of his self-esteem and ego. And let's keep it real, ladies, the reality is most women want their man to be someone they can be proud of and depend on if the going gets tough. And a lot of times this is measured by how successful the guy is in taking care of his family, which in a man's mind equates to "how fat his pocket book is."

The good news, ladies, is that I think a man dealing with commitment avoidance or phobia can overcome this, but it starts with the values he was taught growing up about love, marriage, and respect for women. It also helps if he knows that he has the love and support of a good woman. Men also need to be reassured that being in a relationship is not about giving up their independence but is about sharing a life with someone they love. This means making decisions and working together as equal partners. I also believe that as some men mature they become more responsible, conscious of their actions, and can begin to see the benefits of being in a healthy committed relationship. My only caution, ladies, is that some men take longer to commit than others, if at all; therefore, you may have to ultimately set the limit or know when to draw the line as to how long you are willing to wait for a man to commit to you.

Recap: Ladies...if commitment is what you want from a guy, you have to clearly express this to him, require this from him, and don't compromise how you feel. The more you compromise your feelings, the more you will find yourself frustrated and resenting the guy and the relationship. If a guy cannot give you the commitment you desire, you have to decide if the guy you're with is really the right guy for you. It's just that simple.

CHAPTER 6

How to Tell Your Man the Sex Isn't Good

Let me first ask the question, ladies... how many of you have met a guy and everything was going great until that moment of truth. You finally gave in and he asked, "Who's your daddy?" and in your mind you were thinking... not you! He did not whip it on you or have you walking knock kneed or bow legged after the sex was over. The sex was just not that good. What's worse, you might have committed yourself to a relationship with this guy and don't know how to say, "Um honey, babe, big daddy, your technique can use some serious work."

Well, ladies, the truth is there is no easy way to tell a man that you are sexually unhappy or frustrated because of the sensitive nature of the topic. But when a person's sexual needs are not met, this can easily lead to frustration and even infidelity on the part of the person who is sexually unhappy.

So, first you have to be honest with yourself about how you feel and how you want to be pleased sexually. Quit faking the orgasms, and begin to have dialogue with your man about your true feelings. Now most men have big egos (I will admit!) that can be fragile if they were to hear that they are not satisfying their woman sexually. If it is a matter of your man's level of experience or just not being in sync, there shouldn't be an issue communicating to your man in general terms or in casual conversation how you like to be pleased sexually or things you might like to try.

He should not personalize this and you will be testing the waters to see if he would be open to try some of the things you have suggested. This should not be too threatening to his ego. In fact, he may have had the same thoughts of things he might like to try but was afraid that you would object to whatever he was thinking. You can also experiment by watching adult movies together. He might pick up different tricks to use the next time you guys are doing your thing. Or you can directly tell him that you would like to try some of the things you saw in one of the movies you were watching. This is nothing that a little open dialogue and creativity won't fix, especially if he is open to explore whatever the sexual act is (key words being OPEN TO). You can't force or pressure a man to do things he is not comfortable with, and if this is the case, you might have to ask yourself are you and your man sexually compatible.

Another common issue is a man being too fast on the draw, so to speak. This is a sensitive issue so you have to be very supportive. You first want to assess whether the issue is mental—maybe he gets too excited or maybe he is lacking self-confidence. A suggestion would be to reassure him that you are not going anywhere and be patient with him.

Don't expect a lot the first time you hook up sexually. You should act as though you weren't fazed by his lack of stamina and go to work on getting him aroused again. Each time should increase his stamina. If you seem impatient, disappointed, or turned off from his lack of stamina initially, he will probably feel insecure, inept, and will keep repeating the same mistakes. Sexual confidence with a man is extremely important and cannot be emphasized enough when it comes to a man trying to please a woman. And if all else fails and you don't see an improvement in his sexual stamina, it could possibly be that his issue is physical, in which case you could suggest that he get checked out medically. But again, it is important that he knows he has your support whatever the issue is.

Another very common issue is a man being too rough. If this is the case, you might need to help him take his time or slow things down. There is nothing wrong with a little coaching and developing on your part. Don't pretend by making sounds and love faces and acting as if you enjoy what he is doing if you don't. If he is hurting you or focusing on the wrong places, let him know this and guide him. You might need to remind him that you are different from any woman he has been with, but in a sensitive way. He may be under the impression that his technique always worked before because no one has told him differently, and he may think all women are the same sexually.

The reality is there is no exact blueprint to create good sex in a relationship because of a variety of different factors like chemistry, level of experience, communication, and the individual sexual desires of each person. So achieving sexual satisfaction depends on each individual and may take a little more effort on his and your part. You have to ultimately decide whether you are with someone who has good potential to help you achieve sexual satisfaction.

Also, ladies, don't write a man off just because the first time wasn't as off the chain as you would have liked. With some men it might take a little time, and with some others they'll probably never get it. Having sex for the first time or with a new person can be awkward and clumsy until you get to know each other's sexual style and are comfortable with each other. However, you should hopefully see some improvement or become more in sync as time goes on, IF you are sexually compatible.

In addition, there are some men who have not learned the art of foreplay. If this is important to you, and I believe with most women it is, you may have to educate your man in this area. You can do this is by showing him how it's done i.e. demonstrate on him things you like, or buy books in this area and have them lying around the house and hope that he reads one, or buy videos, which are always good learning tools because you can talk about what you see and like. But ultimately communicating directly how you feel or what you like is the only sure fire way to make sure he clearly understands what you want.

Recap: Sexual satisfaction is a big reason many relationships don't work out. Chemistry, level of experience, communication, and the individual sexual desires of each person are key to achieving sexual satisfaction. So if your needs are not met by your guy, it is very important that you communicate this to him. Being on the same page is extremely important when it comes to having a satisfying love life.

CHAPTER 7

How Long Should You Wait for a Man to Put a Ring on It?

This is another big question I hear from women quite often...

Well, ladies, my response to this is... if you are asking yourself this question, you might have waited too long already. I'm just keepin' it real with you once again...

Yeah it's true, ladies, men are more notorious than women for taking too long to make up their mind about taking the plunge. But in all fairness to men, some women see a potentially good prospect—someone with a good job, good credit, and good benefits—and they instantly want to hog tie him and rush him to the altar. Hmm... you know who you are... already bought your dress, the shoes, and already put the church on reserve. But real talk... I do feel you, ladies... many of you probably believe a good man is hard to find, but you've got to slow it down. This approach will definitely send most men running scared in the opposite direction. Not to mention, you should take as much time as needed to get to know the guy for yourself, even if he seems like he has it all together on the surface...

Biological Clock

I think every woman's clock—biological clock, that is—is different depending on how long she's been dating a guy and depending on her age (usually around thirty plus). Typically this is when a woman starts to really consider settling down, marrying, and having children. So my short answer to how long a woman should wait for her man to put a ring on it should be no longer than what is "reasonable."

What is reasonable is simple, it is when you and your man are in sync about most things (values, beliefs, goals, interests, etc.), have discussed marriage, and it seems like a natural progression to take the relationship to the next level. Of course, this is barring any major issues in the relationship, such as trust or infidelity. If this is the case, I think it would be wise to wait until these issues have been resolved.

Now, ladies, let me break it down further and give you some things to consider in figuring out what is a "reasonable" amount of time for man to put a ring on it. As I said before, you need to ask yourself whether you and your man are in sync about most things. Does the relationship seem to be naturally progressing to the next level? This is spending more time together, learning more things about each other that you like (as well as dislike) and making plans for the future.

On the other hand, you need to ask yourself whether everything seems to be stagnant or forced when it comes to the subject of marriage. By stagnant I mean that your guy is comfortable with keeping things status quo and if you don't bring the subject of marriage up, he will not. By forced I mean always trying to get your man to discuss short or long-term plans of marriage or building a family, and he seems irritated and annoyed when you bring the subject up.

If you find yourself always hinting to your man about marriage or having to constantly ask him, "When is the right time to tie the knot?" he might see this as forcing marriage on him and ultimately he may resent you for it. The truth is you should not have to force your man into marriage. He should see it as an honor and privilege to make you his wife. If the subject of marriage is always evaded or seems taboo, it's probably a safe assumption that your guy may not be on the same page as you. This presents a real issue if this is what you ultimately want from him.

Invested Time

Another thing you might want to consider is the length of time you have been seeing each other exclusively. I would say this is considered invested time—time in which you have more than likely shared personal and intimate information with each other, your hopes and dreams for the future, and possibly engaged in physical intimacy. A woman usually does not take these types of things lightly. In fact, I would venture to say 99.9% of the time a woman in this instance expects that the relationship is progressing well and the guy she's been dating has a very high potential to be the one she'd like to marry someday.

Setting a Timeline

Now let's look at a timeline for a guy to propose. If you and your guy have already discussed marriage, hopefully you have at least set a benchmark or timeline for when you both are considering tying the knot. If the timeline you've discussed seems "reasonable" to you, and the guy's reasoning behind the timeline seems logical (i.e., securing a higher paying job, completing his educational goals and things of this nature), you should be okay with waiting until the time is right as long as you both agree on the terms and continue moving in that direction.

Just keep in mind, ladies, there is a big difference between a guy having a "legitimate" reason for waiting to put a ring on it and a guy making excuses. I use the term "legitimate" because if a guy wants to wait until he earns more money to get married, he should be actively looking for a higher paying job (i.e., pounding the pavement, working on his resume and submitting apps to various jobs). If he is working on completing educational goals, he should be actually going to school and working on some type of vocation or degree.

But whatever it is, I am saying your man's reasoning for delaying marriage should be legitimate and something you can put a finger on or measure. And even if your guy's reasons for waiting to get married are valid, you may still have to decide if the reasons are good enough for you to want to put marriage on hold. Or are the goals you both share something you believe you can work on together as a married couple.

But at the end of the day, ladies, no one can really tell you how long you should wait for your man to put a ring on it because everyone's situation is different. What I have given you are some guidelines and things to consider if you are in this situation. I will also say again, communication is always key to any relationship. You've got to always keep it real with your man about your wants, needs and desires, but most of all keep it real with yourself.

If a ring is what you want, you need to be clear and firm with your man about what you want and don't compromise this. Because the more you compromise what you want, the more you send the message to your man that you're okay with him taking as long as he wants to put a ring on it. And you know what, ladies? The chances are you may never get that ring. If you finally do, you may realize that everything that glitters ain't gold. In other words, do you want your favorite meal presented to you on a platinum, gold or silver platter or do you want it presented to you on a garbage lid? Meaning... did he propose or give you a ring because you are the most precious, beautiful and amazing woman to him or because you pressured and badgered him into submission. Think about it, ladies, is this how you envisioned as a little girl your "prince charming" proposing to you? I'm just saying...

Recap: Ladies... if you know what you want, you need to clearly express this to your guy. And don't compromise this. If it's marriage you want and you've invested a good amount of time getting to know each other, set a reasonable timeline and consider all the pros and cons (compatibility, values, finances, communication, etc.). There should be no reason why you can't get married. But it is important that your guy feels the same way that you do about marriage or you might be wasting a lot of valuable time on the wrong guy. Remember...he should feel like it is an honor and privilege to marry you and not feel as though he was pressured and badgered into submission.

CHAPTER 8

Can Men and Women really be Friends?

"He's just a friend, but you're my man"

Hold up! Hold up! And one more hold up! Now pump the breaks right there, ladies... real talk!

Do you really expect your man to believe you can have a platonic relationship with another guy who's not your man? And you want your man to be cool with that? Alright, let's explore this...

Now you say that you've known your guy friend for a long time. Alright, I can understand that. And you say that your guy friend has been supportive, listens to your problems, and has always been there for you. Okay, I can get with that too. And you say you are only friends with your guy friend but nothing more... Okay, now this is where you've got to pump the breaks and keep it real...

Ladies, I believe that you believe that you can have a guy friend and a man at the same time. And no offense, because I think for the most part your intentions are good and you genuinely want to believe this. On the other hand, some of you are just Bull Sh$@**ing yourselves... let's be real.

In my experience, even if you have maintained a platonic relationship with a guy throughout your friendship, that does not mean there was not the possibility of you and your guy friend hooking up. Just think about it.... maybe there's been some mutual flirting in the past but you never went there because maybe you were always in and out of relationships and only saw your guy friend as a shoulder to lean on in between the breakups? Or, maybe you just were never feelin' your guy friend like that... and he knew this... so he would never go there with you. Trust me, ladies, this does not mean that the thought of you and him hooking up never crossed his mind.

Ladies, if other guys think you got it going on, the chances are your guy friend probably thinks the same. Some men will take on a friendship role if they think that's all they can be, but that does not mean they will not jump at the opportunity if it presents itself. Because the truth is, ladies, MEN DON'T TYPICALLY WANT TO BE JUST FRIENDS... so don't get it twisted... again just keepin' it real. And if the guy friend is secretly diggin' you, he will wait as long as he needs to— months and even years—hoping that one day you will return the feelings.

So my point is, ladies... If your man has expressed that he has an issue with you having other male friends or one close male friend in particular, he may have a point. Men will be men and men know how other men think and operate. I don't mean to generalize all men, but I'm just keepin' it real. Do I think trust in a relationship is important? No doubt! Should your guy trust you? I say absolutely... unless, you have given him a reason to doubt you. Should your man trust the other guy? Hell-to-the-naw!

Seriously... people make mistakes with the best intentions. We are human with human flaws. Like I said... even if you are not feelin' the guy friend, it does not mean he is not feelin' you in that way. All it takes is a few too many drinks and a vulnerable moment that can lead to a slip and fall that you never intended or saw coming. Remember, to a large degree, you're already emotionally connected to this guy that you consider your friend, and for women this type of connection means a LOT.

Some Definite NO-NOs...

Ladies, if you currently have a man, a definite no-no is that first you should not be discussing intimate details of your relationship with another guy (family member excluded—although you really should be talking to the person you're in the relationship with about any concerns you might have if at all possible). Second, you should not be looking to another guy for emotional support if you are having problems in your relationship. And finally, you should not be spending a lot of time with another guy who's not your man (i.e., lunch, shopping, movies, dinner, etc.) or always talking privately on the phone, texting, Instagramming, or face-timing. This is disrespectful to your man and crosses boundaries that can definitely lead to some big-time problems in your relationship.

J-watt's Food for Thought...

Let me leave you with some food for thought. If your man is truly giving you everything you need in the relationship, why do you need or desire these same things from your so-called guy friend? Also, if your friend truly cares about you and respects you, he will respect your relationship and step back. This does not always mean that you have to stop being friends altogether. It just means that you may have to redefine how the friendship will be. And in some cases, it may be necessary to cut off the friendship if you really value your relationship with your man.

You also need to be real with yourself and ask yourself are you hanging on to your guy friend out of fear that your relationship won't work out. One suggestion on how to play it safe is if you genuinely care about your relationship and want it to work, you may want to consider hanging out with other couples or mutual friends. And if you want to maintain a friendship with other people independent of your relationship, a suggestion would be to make sure that your man knows the other person and is cool with it... REALLY COOL WITH IT.

It's definitely not a good idea to be keeping secrets in the relationship, and if you feel you have to do this, it is probably a sign that something is wrong with the relationship or you are diggin' the other person more than you are letting on. Again, ladies, and the same goes for men, communicate with each other so you don't get caught up and lose a good thing.

Recap: Ladies...if you are starting a new relationship and already have an existing guy friend, it's good to make sure you establish clear boundaries with your guy friend. You also want to make sure the guy you're in the relationship with is cool with the friendship. A true friend will respect your relationship and want you to be happy. And you always want to make sure that you are open and honest with both parties about the role they play in your life.

CHAPTER 9

What Men Say and Do to Get Women in Bed

Real talk, ladies... the truth is most men will say and do just about anything to get you in bed. No surprise there... right? Well, this is a common characteristic most men share. It's just in a man's nature, generally speaking, to be the pursuer when it comes to women. And believe me when I tell you it's not your mind or your personality that a man wants when he first sets eyes on you. So please don't get it twisted and think that you're special in that way... no offense, ladies. Although deeper qualities about a woman will or may come into play later, men are men and ultimately men want what a woman has... and that is the Cali Poppy, the Kitty Kat, the Cookie, the Vajayjay, the Ill Na Na, the Punani, or whatever term refers to that part of the female anatomy that drives men absolutely crazy. I tell women all the time that you really have the control in how the relationship will go (at least in the beginning when meeting a guy) and don't even realize it. I'll speak more on that later.

Hey, Girl... That Must be Jelly because Jam Don't Shake like That

A man saying just about anything to get a woman's attention is not a new phenomenon. Some men use what is called "game" or "lines" as a prelude to ultimately trying to get a woman in bed. In fact, depending on your age, you might have heard old school "playa's" use the line "Hey, baby... what's your sign?" Others might have heard lines like "Girl, you look so fine, I'll drink your bath water," or "Girl, you must be tired because you've been running through my mind all day," or the classic line "Don't I know you from somewhere."

While these lines might seem corny and tired and don't work on all or most women, they have been known to work for some men in their pursuit of getting what they want from a woman. On the other hand, some women require men to be far more imaginative with their game or approach, so men are always inventing new things to say or do to get what they want. Some men are also very good at just employing the natural, genuine approach. But at the end of the day, lines or no lines, real, natural or genuine is all a man's way of trying to get the woman they want in bed.

Hey, Sexy, Let Me Buy You a Drink...

Men will also do just about anything to get women in bed. Some men will do things like buying a woman a drink or taking her out to dinner or to a movie as a precursor to getting her in bed. Other men will be far more cunning and manipulative like showering a woman with expensive material things or taking her on whirlwind trips to make her feel obligated to give him sexual favors in return.

The ultimate manipulation is a guy guilt tripping a woman into believing that if she does not have sex with him, she does not really love or care about him. This makes it very hard for a woman to resist his wishes, so be extremely careful of a guy employing this tactic, especially, ladies, if you just met the guy or have only known him a short time. Make sure that a man's actions match his words before you give up what's in your secret garden.

The natural concern for you, ladies, is that it is not always easy to detect what a man's intentions are in the beginning. Does he just want to get you in bed or does he see you beyond a sexual relationship? Well here are some things to consider that might help you discern what a man's intentions are beyond just getting you in bed.

Some men may be direct and let you know up front exactly what they want...this type of guy's intentions are pretty clear. If he is a DECENT guy, this will be done tastefully. Ladies, you shouldn't be offended by this. It doesn't necessarily mean the guy doesn't respect you or thinks you are easy. He wants to be open and honest because he does respect you, and you should appreciate knowing the rules that you are playing by or what you might be getting yourself into.

Usually this takes a very secure and mature man because the risk of a woman misinterpreting his intentions and turning him down are high. In my opinion, I think if a guy is truthful about what he wants, you both can be clear about the expectations of the relationship... whether or not it will just be a sexual relationship or something more. My only caution to you, ladies, is—if you agree in the beginning to just having a sexual relationship, you cannot flip the script later and try to change the terms. You really have to be honest with yourself and the guy as to whether you can handle this type of relationship.

On the other hand, the most "common" type of guy is not so direct about what he really wants. The main reason is because this type of guy has learned that women typically do not favor this type of approach and he knows he might not get what he wants if he is completely honest. This is not a "good" or "bad" type of guy necessarily. It is just difficult for a woman to know what his real intentions are until the relationship progresses. He might listen to all your problems, wine and dine you, buy you material things, laugh at your jokes (even if they are bad), eat your biscuits (even if they're burnt), spend time with your kids (even if they are bad as hell), and tell you all the things you want to hear to get you in bed.

For some women they may prefer this type of guy to the former because they want to fool themselves into believing that this type of guy is better somehow if he comes across as though he is less preoccupied with sex or respects women more... uh, not so true. The fact is with this type of a guy, a woman has to be more direct in her questioning about his intentions, read the subtle cues as to whether he seems genuinely interested in her as a person, determine if there is good chemistry with the guy, and ultimately rely on her instincts and best judgment about the guy.

I also strongly suggest that you don't ignore, dismiss or overlook any red flags. These are usually signs that prove to be spot on later on down the line. Some examples of red flags that shouldn't be ignored or dismissed are a guy coming on too strongly in trying to get you to sleep with him, especially if you just met. Saying he loves you rolls off his lips too easily, but he doesn't call or text you for a while, if at all, after having sex. He seems hot and cold when you do talk to him (i.e., seeming to click one minute and seeming annoyed and distant at other times), or he only calls or texts you when he wants a "booty call." Or, maybe he only wants to kick it with you in secluded places or at his convenience.

Panty Rule...

Some women also believe that it is necessary to put a strict timeline on when they will let a man sleep with them. In my opinion, this does not really work because it comes across as playing games, and a sexual relationship should flow naturally. And as I said before, some men will wait as long as it takes to get what they want. All men have some idea of how long they are willing to play the game.

If you want to get to know more about a guy first or you believe in saving yourself before marriage because of your values or religious beliefs, be honest about why you want to wait. Trust me, ladies, a man (if he is a GOOD man) will appreciate and respect you for your honesty and the fact that you are not playing games. And again, if he is a good man, he will stick around and wait until you are ready to be intimate with him or let you know where he stands.

On the other hand, if you decide to be sexual with a guy sooner than later, it is important to be CLEAR about what you want or expect from that sexual relationship (i.e., no strings attached or a commitment) to avoid any confusion or misunderstandings on your part. It is up to the guy to do the same. If he is a good man, he will.

Understand, ladies... playing the strict "panty rule" game is not a one-hundred-percent guarantee that a guy will respect you or stick around after he gets what he wants. The truth is in some cases a guy might resent the fact that a woman made him wait so long and take off as soon as he gets what he wants. And, ladies... you can best believe that while a guy is waiting out your timeline... he is more than likely getting his needs met elsewhere...again, just keepin' it real.

Bottom line is... the choice to enter into a sexual relationship with a man is definitely yours to make, but this should be done with your eyes WIDE open. And as I mentioned at the beginning of this chapter, ladies, you ultimately have the control to take it slow or fast and set the terms of the relationship because a man wants what you have. If you need to ask questions, ask them. If something seems off, follow your instincts and best judgment. DON'T IGNORE THE OBVIOUS SIGNS.

That said, I don't think there's anything wrong with giving in to a man sexually if it fits within your belief system, you are informed about his intentions, and you have at least gotten to know some basic information about the guy. You also want to be clear about the expectations of the relationship, ensure you both agree on whatever the terms are, and be certain you are both mature, responsible people.

And if you find a guy who is open and honest about what he wants and is able to communicate his wants in a respectable manner, these are always good qualities in a man to consider. But at the end of the day, I think waiting until you feel you're absolutely sure or ready to be sexual with a guy gives you the best chance for your relationship to work out that much better.

Recap: It's true...men have sex on the brain most of the time and will say and do just about anything to get it. But it is a woman's prerogative to decide who she wants to be sexually intimate with and when she is ready. Remember, ladies... you have the control to go as fast or slow as you want, but it's always good to wait until you're absolutely sure you're ready. And if you're not ready to be sexually intimate, be honest. You don't want a guy to think that you're playing games by giving mixed signals, and if he's a good guy, he will respect you more for your honesty.

CHAPTER 10

The Art of Playing Cat and Mouse with a Man

Ladies... I wouldn't suggest playing a lot of games with a man as a general rule, but playing a little cat and mouse can be an exception to that rule. Some games can be healthy for a relationship, but the truth is there is a fine line. Too many games can be a definite turn off. And you have to be careful, ladies, because if you're playing the game of too hard to get, you might not get got. You can also miss out on a good thing. But I think in the beginning a woman should play a little hard to get because most men like the challenge and excitement of the chase.

Now obviously some men purposely seek women who are easy, no fuss, no fight, what are you doing to night and can I come over. But generally speaking, men prefer women who will present a little challenge. Most men by nature and nurture like to chase and then to conquer as the saying goes... this is only after the woman has allowed herself to be conquered of course. (Don't worry, ladies, I got you covered). But seriously... if it is too easy, where's the excitement in that?

Not to mention, most men typically do not have the highest regard for women who are too easy... that's just keepin' it real. It is said, "The fruit that is farther from the tree is better than the fruit that falls at your feet." So, ladies, even if you meet a guy you think is really hot, there is nothing wrong with taking it slow and allowing the man to pursue you.

You never want to come off as desperate, overly aggressive, or stalker-ish. This type of behavior will definitely scare away most guys. I'm not telling you to completely ignore a guy and expect that he will somehow know that you are interested in him, or expect that he will break his neck chasing you even if you believe that you got it going on. It's about playing the game of cat and mouse—you give a little, and he reciprocates, and so on.

The Flirting Game

Now, ladies... if you are not sure what kind of vibe you are getting from a guy, a good way to find this out is by flirting with him (this is especially important if he's a shy or reserved type of guy). This will also let a guy know you are interested in him without being too aggressive or too forward. Some of the ways to get a guy's attention without doing too much include things like giving him a nice friendly greeting (hi or hello), a wink, a smile, eye contact, being playful, or you can compliment him on how he looks.

There is nothing wrong with giving a guy signals. You just have to find a balance between not giving a guy any vibe or signals (a common mistake that many women make) to coming on too strong and either scarring a guy off or leading him to believe that you are "easy." In other words, you don't have to go out of your way, or some might call this "putting a 20 on a 10," to make him notice you.

Trust me, ladies, if a guy is really interested in you, he will pick up on the signals and reciprocate in a way that should be clear he is interested. And it's not about being an old-school or a new-school type of woman, but basic flirting with a guy lets him know that you are a woman who knows what you want and you are not afraid to let it be known. It also tells a guy that you are not above approach (conceded or stuck up). The idea is to use that natural feminine charm you are born with, and let the man do the rest.

Exchanging Numbers

Now, ladies...exchanging numbers with a guy is important because it sets the tone of the first contact with a guy and his impression of you. So if you are exchanging telephone numbers for the first time (unless you take his number because you are being cautious), you do not have to call or text him right away. Give him a chance to pursue you (again, there's nothing wrong with being a little old fashion that way). It's good to keep a guy guessing. This also keeps a guy stimulated and intrigued.

Now once he calls you, you can return his call. If he is unavailable or misses your call, you should give him time to respond to your returned call. Multiple calls can definitely send the wrong message and may start a guy thinking that you are desperate or needy. The same thing applies if you've been out on a couple of dates with a guy. You don't want to start blowing up his phone because he has not made you the center of his world as you probably expected or hoped.

This is a definite NO-NO! Again if a man is really feelin' you... and I mean REALLY feelin' you... trust me when I tell you he will pursue you. I want to really emphasize this because some women get caught up in playing the "what if" and "why" game. You know... what if he does not like me or why hasn't he called.

Again, ladies, don't try to force it. Just let it flow naturally, and a guy will let it be known that he is interested—if he is really interested. And just because a man does not call you right away does not mean he is not feelin' you. He could actually be busy (this is a good thing if he works or attends school or is doing something else productive with his time—key word is PRODUCTIVE). It could also be his way of playing cat and mouse with you. Whatever the case, give the man some time to make the first move. A day or two before he calls you is not unreasonable.

Keep Doing You...

This is a common mistake that many women make after they get a man. Ladies, you cannot let your friends go or stop doing things that you are interested in because you want to spend all of your time with your new man. Most men do not like being totally depended upon or overly crowded. Nor, ladies, do you want to lose your own independence. If you enjoy doing things like going shopping with your girlfriends, spa treatments, or rock climbing (I don't want to be presumptuous), don't stop. Just keep doing you.

Make sure your man still knows that he comes first but recognizes that you still have a life too. A man likes to see that his woman has other things going on besides him. This is definitely a turn on and will probably draw him closer to you and make him want to spend more time with you—if that's what you ultimately want. This is just a little reverse psychology, ladies, to get a man to do what you want without you having to directly tell him. If you're doing all these things and he is still not giving you enough time, the direct approach is always the best.

I Already Got My Man, So Why Do I have to Continue to Play Cat and Mouse?

Another important thing to know, ladies, is that playing the game of cat and mouse does not stop just because you've got your man. You still have to keep things exciting. It's good to mix it up from time to time, like sending your man his favorite chocolates with a note to meet you at a secret location for lunch or after work. The secret place can be any place where the two of you can be alone to do whatever comes to mind.

This might be a good time to pull out that lingerie you've been saving or greet him wearing an overcoat with nothing underneath. You can also send your man slightly risqué pictures of yourself while he's at work or out with the guys (although this really depends on your trust and comfort level, especially nowadays when a private picture can spread all over the internet). This should give him something to think about and make him want to hurry home to you. But it doesn't always have to be sexual. In fact, sending your man a simple text or email on occasions just to let him know you love him, miss him, and appreciate him goes a very long way and will definitely keep him chasing you. You do not want things to get stale or boring. The idea is to keep him guessing and on his toes.

Recap: Whether you you're trying to land a man or keep a man, there is nothing wrong with playing a little cat and mouse. Most guys like the challenge and excitement of the chase. This keeps the relationship exciting and new.

CHAPTER 11

Why Do Some Women Get Labeled Freaks, Sluts, Hoes and Tricks?

Ladies... this chapter is not meant to offend you, but you know I got to keep it real with you as I always do. Real talk... when a man refers to a woman as a freak, slut, hoe, or trick, it has everything to do with the way she carries herself. Now I don't condone men labeling or judging women in this way, but the truth is there is still a very strong male perception about how a woman should behave or carry herself... simply put men want a "good girl" in the streets by their and everyone else's perception but a freak in the bedroom.

A "good girl" is essentially a woman a man can feel proud of—someone he can show off to his homeboys, someone he can take home to meet his mother, and ultimately someone he sees as a potential wife. This type of girl knows how to dress sexy and classy but not trashy. This type of girl knows how to act like a lady in public and essentially set it off in the bedroom.

Conversely, men have used terms like freak, slut, hoe and trick to describe women they feel don't fit their idea of a "good girl." And don't believe for a minute that a guy would never label you because he said he loves you or you think he is different... WRONG! Let me tell you, men go hard, sometimes harder than women with their gossip and telling stories about their latest conquest.

If this does not matter to you or your reputation, keep doing what you do, but there is a saying that you can't make a "hoe" a housewife. The way a woman carries herself determines how she is perceived by a man. Here are some examples of things a woman might do that could get her labeled a freak, slut, hoe or trick.

Let me break it down...

A woman having frequent sexual encounters with different men and not being in a committed relationship with any of these men could get her labeled. Essentially, most men do not want a woman that is considered to be used goods... someone who has been around the block on more than a few occasions. A man generally likes to view his woman as "innocent" or "virtuous" although this is probably an unfair and unrealistic view. Men have a very hard time imagining their woman having been with one man let alone several men sexually. So, ladies, my suggestion is don't be eager to volunteer too much information (TMI) about your past exploits. The fact is psychologically men can't really handle this type of truth. Less is generally best!

Slow it down, ladies...

Giving up the Cali Poppy too soon can also get a woman labeled. This is a hard fact, ladies, when it comes to how men view women because some women unfairly get a bad rap when they are only doing what men have always done... exploring their feminine wiles and oats.

But unfortunately, even in today's age, it is still not viewed the same way. As I said before, I think a sexual relationship should flow naturally, but you have to be extra careful if you decide to have a casual hook up or give up your Cali Poppy too soon because not every guy is mature enough to handle this type of sexual encounter. And trust me, ladies... this type of guy will go back and tell his homeboys in a hurry that he got with you and you gave it up on the first date or soon after you met.

The guy might also wonder how many other guys have you given it up to the same way, which might diminish any chance of being with this guy if you decide you really want a relationship with him later on. On the other hand, do I think having a thirty, sixty or ninety-day panty rule is the answer? No, I don't. This may backfire and a guy may feel you're playing games and resent you for it.

However, I think is it is always good to know more about a man before you give up the goods because it increases the chance of you having a positive sexual experience versus a not so good experience. Men are also built to deal with a casual hook up better than women emotionally... again meaning that men can generally detach from a sexual relationship easier than a woman. Women also have to be careful because some guys might not detach so easily. You could have a stalker, a guy who is very possessive, or someone who might have violent tendencies on your hands. So obviously the more time you take to get to know a guy before you hook up with him sexually, the better you know what you are dealing with.

Com' On, Not the Homie...

Smashing the homie is another sure fire way to get a woman labeled. This is a definite no-no, ladies. A man does not want to know that his woman has been with any of his friends sexually. Again the visual is too much for a man to fathom. Not to mention it is extremely embarrassing for that man and his ego, knowing all of his homeboys know that his lady smashed one of the homies. Again, ladies, men talk and gossip just as much as women do.

Do Clothes Make the Woman?

A woman dressing too racy or provocative is another way to get her labeled. How a woman dresses has a lot to do with how a man views her and will ultimately treat her. As I said before, men are visual and are attracted to what they see. And if a woman has her breasts overly exposed, overly tight clothes, dresses or skirts that are too short, provocative piercing or tattoos, and always flaunting her body... there's no doubt a man will be after her like she was the last pork chop on the plate.

But keep in mind, ladies, a man probably has already perceived that woman as easy and someone who might get around whether this is true or not. And once a guy views a woman this way, it's hard for him to see beyond the exterior to deeper qualities she might possess (i.e., how smart she is, that she has a good sense humor, or that she's a good person). Now how you dress is a personal choice—I get it.

And you will definitely get a lot of attention if you are scantily dressed, but in more cases than not, you will be attracting the wrong type of attention. There is nothing wrong with giving a guy a little preview of the upcoming attraction so to speak, but you don't want to give away the preview, plot, and ending at first sight. In other words, there is a way to be classy and sexy in style and dress without putting it all out there. There is also a time and place for everything... meaning that you might not want to wear those booty shorts and knee high boots to work, school, or the supermarket, but this might be okay if you are going to a club. And even still, you may find yourself getting a lot of attention but from the wrong type of guys. Here's a little tip about men, ladies... most men like it when a woman leaves something to the imagination and to be seen by him only.

Following a Man's Lead...

Being too experienced or seeming too freaky too soon could also get a woman labeled. This is a tough one, ladies... very much like sleeping with a man too soon. I know I said a man wants a "lady" in the streets and a "freak" in the bed, BUT not when you first meet a guy. You have to be careful... there is a fine line in how much you give up too soon and this has to be handled carefully, with finesse and good judgment.

As I said before, a lot of men like the image of a "good girl," that is if they see a woman as a potential MAIN woman in their life or possible marriage material. Again, men do not want to hear all of a woman's past exploits; hence, they do not want a woman who is too experienced or too freaky in the bedroom right off. In other words, if it is your first time hooking up with a man sexually, you don't need to try to impress him by throwing everything you've learned before you met him at him all at once.

A good example of a woman doing way too much is going "down" on a guy when she first meets him or sleeps with him. Ladies... it's like the fruit flavored candy "Now and Later," that many of us enjoyed as kids. Give a little taste now and save the best for later. Now of course a man will NEVER object to getting everything a woman has to offer sexually, but it will certainly raise his eyebrows and get him thinking... DAMN... how many other men has she been with sexually, or this girl is a freak! In some cases you may have to curtail what you know initially until you get a feel for what a man knows or likes. I'm not saying do not participate in the sexual experience, but follow his lead and as you get to know his pace or sexual style, then you can gradually bring more of your experience into the sexual relationship.

This is not to say that you must do everything he wants you to either. You have to be somewhat discriminate in what you do initially. But all in all... most men like to feel as though they are doing the teaching (although this is not to say that some men don't mind being the student). Again you have to assess this and make this determination based on getting to know your man (and there's nothing wrong with asking a man what he likes directly). The way a man views how much experience a woman has or how freaky she is sexually may also vary depending on her age. Obviously if a woman is thirty plus, there may be a different expectation in that she comes with a certain amount of experience. A good rule would be—if you have not been married, would like to be married, and are under thirty, I would suggest considering the "Now and Later" approach.

J-watt's Rules of Thumb

If more than one guy from the same circle can say, "Yeah, man, I slept with her too," there is a problem. If more than one guy from the same circle can describe your tattoo or birthmark in the most private area in detail, or talk about the pimple on your booty, there is a problem. If more than one guy can say, "She let me hit it on the first date or soon after we met," then you have a problem.

If more than one guy can describe the exact time your father or mother goes to work or to sleep or the color of your sheets, then you definitely have a problem. If you have to use your fingers and toes to count how many men you've been with sexually, I would say without a doubt this is a problem. I'm just saying... these are some things that might get a woman labeled a freak, slut, hoe or trick!

If you got it going on, ladies, and you are confident, you don't have to put it all out there. A "real" man will know the deal. Be smart, ladies!

Recap: The way a woman carries herself will ultimately determine how a man will perceive her and treat her...REAL TALK!

CHAPTER 12

He Says One Thing and Does Another

Ladies... I know you would like to believe and trust what a man is telling you is real... especially if he's telling you all the things you want to hear like how beautiful you are, or that you are the only one for him, or that he loves you. And while there might be some degree of truth to what he is telling you, you really have to take his words with a grain of salt, at least until you have reason to believe otherwise.

In other words, you should not believe everything a man tells you without some reservations. I am not saying that you should not trust men or that all men lie, but some men have become VERY GOOD at telling women what they want to hear to get what they want. And unfortunately, ladies, some of you have made men telling you what you want to hear extremely easy to do... no offense. But generally speaking women have a very trusting nature when it comes to men.

Like R. Kelly said, "Y'all love us so much our lies become the truth." Women treat men as innocent until proven guilty when it should be the complete opposite. You really should reserve your judgment until you have gathered enough concrete evidence to prove that what a man is telling you is true. There are two ways to find out if a man is really being honest with you—over time and, more importantly, through his actions.

Think about it, ladies... how can you tell if a girlfriend is worthy of your trust? This is done by getting to know her over time and by her track record. Men are no different. If a man says he loves you, he should also demonstrate this by his actions (i.e., spending quality time with you, giving you his undivided attention, returning your phone calls in a timely manner, respecting you, putting your needs first, being open and honest with you, compromising, being supportive, and being dependable to name a few).

These things should also be consistent over time, not just when you first meet a guy and he is saying and doing all the right things. Conversely, if a man says he loves you and is not showing you in any of the previously mentioned ways, you need to run the other way faster than an Olympic track star and never look back...seriously. And, ladies, the sooner you recognize that a guy's behavior is not matching what he is telling you, the sooner you can keep it movin' and avoid getting sucked into his very skillful and manipulative web of lies.

In other words, be decisive early in the relationship about moving on before you get caught up emotionally. It's not that complicated, ladies... you just have to be smart and see things for what they really are and not what you want them to be. Do not be blinded by what you think are good looks, nice physique, money, status, or charm. You really should look deeper than the cover and read every page carefully to get a complete picture of a man.

Again, do not ignore the obvious signs or red flags. Do not make excuses for why a man does certain things. Bottom line—if a man's actions are consistent with his words, you do not have to make excuses, figure out, or wonder if he is telling you the truth or means what he says. It will be obvious!

Recap: Like the old adage says, "Don't believe everything you hear," especially if it's a man whispering sweet nothings in your ear. I added the "sweet nothings" because in some cases that's just what it is, nothing that means you any good. The truth is not all guys want to be dishonest or omit certain facts, but men have been conditioned to believe that honesty doesn't always get them what they want. And some guys are really skilled at telling you what you want to hear. So, ladies, don't be afraid to ask a man as many questions as you need to get to know him better. And if you have some reservations about the guy or what he is telling you, it's better to be decisive early about moving on than later. Remember... trust is something that is earned and should not be given freely.

CHAPTER 13

Eleven Things You Want to Know When You First Meet a Guy

Ladies...don't be scurd ... uh, uh... don't be scurd (translation...don't be scared) to ask a man questions. But more importantly, you want to ask the RIGHT questions. This is real talk... some women ask more questions when they are buying shoes or a dress or trying to decide about getting their hair or nails done than they do when they are dating a man. You know what I'm talking about, ladies... well that's not good.

There is nothing wrong with asking a man questions, and if he is a "real" man, he will have no problem answering your questions. Contrary to popular belief... a "real" man should be able to handle a mature, adult conversation without being intimidated or scared off by you asking him questions. I'm not saying pull out your clipboard and checklist on the first date or interrogate a brotha like you're the police... I'm just saying you can ask the need-to-know questions through casual conversation.

This can be done on that first or even the second date, if you do not want to blast a guy with too many questions all at once. And you will stand a better chance of having a guy answer your questions when you first meet him because ... why? He wants you... simply put... and this is a rare occasion when you can get a guy to do almost anything.

Now... why is asking a guy the RIGHT questions important? It is important because it will save you from wasting a lot of valuable time and from potential frustration and heartache later on in the relationship... and this is real talk. I will give you eleven things you should know when you first meet a guy. This is not an exhaustive list by any means or in any particular order, but these BASIC questions will help lay the foundation on which you can build when you first meet a guy or help you decide if you need to move on...

1. ***Knowing a man's education and/or intellectual level*** – This is good to learn about a man because you want to know if intellectually you are compatible. It's just not enough for a man to be "easy on the eyes" because trust me, ladies, this will get old eventually. I say educational and/or intellectual level because a man does not have to have a degree necessarily to be intelligent. But in most cases, education does signify a certain intellectual level. And his intellect should match yours.

The fact is most women are cerebral and need to be stimulated mentally. If a man cannot articulate himself, communicate effectively, or hold a conversation on different levels, this will create a lot frustration in the relationship. For example, if you like to have deep-meaning conversations, talk about social ills in the world, politics, or religion and a man's only conversation is discussing what's for dinner or who Lil Wayne is sleeping with, this will present an issue.

It can also present issues around misunderstandings and misinterpretations in the relationship. A man's educational/ intellectual level might also indicate whether he is good at thinking logically, has good reasoning, or has the ability to compromise when it comes to concepts like managing finances or child rearing practices. Another important thing to note is that if there is incompatibility in education or intellect, this often times can bring about jealousy or envy in the relationship. Men especially have a hard time dealing with this concept.

2. ***Is he secure financially*** – Knowing whether a guy is financially secure is important, especially if you yourself are financially independent. Too often women dummy down or settle for a man who is not equally yoked financially. This can present a problem on many levels and obviously finances are a big part of any relationship. Let's keep it real... love alone will not pay the bills.

A woman being the breadwinner can cause resentment on her part if she has to always "buy the food and fry it up in the pan" so to speak. Most men also still struggle with not being able to provide for the family in the way that they want to when they're not financially secure. Financial security and being a good provider is still very important to a male's manhood in terms of his self-esteem. This can cause frustration on the man's part and ultimately strain the relationship.

3. ***Is he ambitious and does he have goals*** – Finding out if a man is ambitious and has goals speaks to whether he is a "go getter" or not. For some women this is important when they are looking for a potential husband. Essentially if a guy has ambition and goals, he will likely have a certain degree of confidence about himself and be better prepared to handle the responsibilities of a family. But too much ambition without balance is not good either. It is important for a man to understand that while being a good provider and having a good career are important, these qualities should not be seen

as the most important in life, especially if they supersede you or the relationship.

4. ***Does he like children*** – This is important to know about a man, especially if you're husband hunting and hope to have children someday. This is also important if you already have a child and want to know if the man you meet will accept your child. It can help you gauge how well your child will respond to him as well. For most women this is a deal breaker. You need to know this up front before you become too emotionally invested with any guy.

5. ***Does he already have children*** – If a man already has a child, it would be VERY important to know what kind of relationship he has with his child (i.e., does he spend quality time with his child and does he provide for his child financially). The way a man takes care of his responsibilities says a lot about his character. If a man is stepping up to the plate and taking care of his responsibilities, this is commendable and, ladies, you need to support him and continue to encourage him to do the right thing.

He will appreciate you for supporting him versus resenting you for not. Also, the way a man deals with his child's mother will tell you something about how he is able to handle a potentially complicated situation. If his relationship with his child's mother is not ideal, is he able to put the child's needs first and make every effort to try to co-parent with that mother.

Yes, some "baby mamas" try to make it very difficult for a man to do the right thing when it comes to taking care of his children. But it is very important for you to know that he is making a solid effort to take care of his responsibilities, and this sets a good example for that child.

6. **_Is he close to his mother_** – Finding out whether a man is close to his mother is very important. Typically how a man relates to his mother is how he views women in general and how he will ultimately treat a woman. If a man respects his mother and has received care and nurturing from his mother, he will tend to have a sensitive and caring nature when it comes to women.

It is also important to know if a guy is overly close with his mother and has trouble cutting the cord as an adult. This type of guy is known as a "Mama's Boy." The difference between the two is that one understands his role as an independent adult man and is able to put his woman's needs first.

The Mama's Boy has not been able to successfully separate from his mother's influence and will find it very difficult to put his woman's needs first. This type of guy might also struggle with having a mature, equitable adult relationship. In other words, he will seek out a woman who represents a mother figure and not someone who will be an equal partner. This is okay if you are looking for man to take care of, someone who has not fully matured as an adult and still needs some parenting. With this type of guy, you might also be setting yourself up for lots of conflict between the guy and his mother with you in the middle as you try to establish your place in his life.

7. **_What is a guy's living situation_** – This is important because it can signify where a man might be in his maturity, financial independence, and in some cases reveal if he is single or attached. If a guy still lives at home... you might want

to know with whom and why is he still living at home depending on his age. If a guy is still living at home in his 20s, this might be reasonably understandable if he is working on his education or saving money to get his own place. As I said, this question may also tell you if a man is single or is living with another woman.

Of course you will need to ask more questions and probably see for yourself what a guy's living situation is to know for sure whether he is single or not, but asking this question is a good start. If a guy is in his 30s and he is still living at home, you might want to know what has prevented him from getting his own apartment or house (i.e., credit problems, poor money management, lack of ambition, loss of a job, divorce, child support, etc.).

8. ***Does he have domestic skills*** – This may not be a deal breaker or requirement for some women; however, this is good to know if you want a man that will help in sharing the household responsibilities. If a man is comfortable with domestic work, he will usually chip in around the house with no problem and not feel as though it is the woman's job to do all the work.

Sometimes when the household work is not equitable, this may cause some resentment on the woman's part as she might not feel totally appreciated. Also very important, ladies... you don't want to mislead your man in thinking that you're okay with doing all the domestic work, especially if you are really not cool with it because he may come to expect this. Some women set themselves up to fail in this way because they think this is the way to snag a man or husband, but this will only backfire, ladies, and cause greater problems in the long run.

9. ***What are his interest/hobbies*** – This is important to know because you want to know if you share some things in common. Trust me, ladies... this will definitely come in to play if you enjoy traveling, dancing, going to the movies, or out to dinner and your guy is a couch potato and only likes to play video games or watch sports all day. In most cases this tiger will not change his stripes and you will have issues with this.

You don't have to share everything in common, but it is important to have some things in common that you both can enjoy together. I would also add that you should be open to learn some of his other interests that are not in common. This will go a long way in making the relationship even stronger.

This definitely goes both ways as a relationship is about give and take and compromise. You do not have to like all of the same things to still spend time together doing what the other person likes to do. It's easy to do something you both like, but it takes more effort to do something you don't necessarily like. He should appreciate your efforts and vice versa.

10. ***Is he Spiritual or Religious*** – This question may not be important for everyone depending on your spiritual or religious beliefs. But for some, it is important because religion and/or spirituality may play a key role in a man's values and beliefs about life and love (i.e., do you share the same belief about sex before marriage, child rearing practices, who will wear the pants in the household, or even celebrating holidays like Christmas or Kwanza). If you are also religious and/or spiritual, you would want to know if you are compatible in this way. The closer you are spiritually and/or share the same religious beliefs, the better chance you have in developing a good relationship and maintaining it.

11. ***What are his intentions with you*** – This is probably at the top of the list of questions that most fathers would ask a guy dating their daughter... usually for good reason! But this is a good question for you to ask a guy yourself. One, you want to see how well he thinks on his feet by how he answers the question because he will be caught off guard initially.

If he is stumbling and bumbling, obviously he has not given much thought to a relationship, thus why is he trying to hook up with you? Does he just want the sex? Two, this is a good open-ended question meaning that a guy can say whatever comes to mind, but it is your job to take the information and judge for yourself whether he says what he thinks you want to hear.

Some guys are real charmers and smooth, so you have to be careful if his answer is on point. With the smooth guy, you may need to ask follow up questions to discern whether he is being genuine and keeping it real with you. But the idea of asking this question is that it opens the door for you to get more information to decide if you want to continue dating a particular guy.

Now, ladies... this is not an exhaustive list by any means as mentioned. But these are solid basic questions that I think are very important to learn when you first meet a guy. You may have other questions you want to ask a guy that are also important to you. But my point is—don't ever be afraid to ask a guy questions because this will not hurt you. Not asking questions or the RIGHT questions can potentially hurt you. And remember a guy is more inclined to answer your questions up front when everything is new and fresh than later when he feels he has more control over the relationship.

By that time you're already emotionally invested. It's harder to back out of a relationship than it is to get into one.

In the back of this book, I have listed other questions that you might want to make note of and ask a guy. More importantly though, I encourage you to make a list of things that you want in a guy. If you find a guy who has at least eighty percent (meaning at least eight out of ten) of the things you are looking for, I think this is a very good start. But keep in mind, ladies, no one will have everything you want and you also need to know that you are probably not going to have everything he wants. But this is okay because no one is perfect.

Recap: This chapter listed eleven things that every woman should learn when first getting to know a man. These basic things will lay the foundation a woman can build upon when she first meets a guy or help her decide if she needs to move on.

Ladies... if you try to build a relationship on a shaky foundation, chances are that relationship will crumble.

CHAPTER 14

What Makes a Man Fall in Love and How Do You Know?

Ladies... if you are asking yourself this question or want to know if the man you are with loves you, I'm going to let you know the real.

The truth is I don't think men are that different than women in what makes them fall in love. The basic difference between men and women is most men are not going door to door looking for love, whereas, I think women tend to seek love out. In other words, men do not have the mindset that each new girl they meet is that potential love mate. This is something that just happens to men as they are dating, like the proverbial saying "Getting hit over the head with a sledge hammer." It just hits them when they least expect it most of the time.

Now what makes a man fall in love when he meets that "special" woman is just that... she is special because she is different from any other women he has ever known. She is able to stand out from the crowd. But she is not different because she is trying to be, she is different because she is being herself.

She is true to herself, not pretentious, fake or phony. What makes a woman stand out from the crowd can be summed up in one word "real." I'll break this down for you, ladies, to give you a better idea of what I mean by "real." Now you should be pretty familiar with this term because it's a term that I used throughout this book... keepin' it real.

It's about being genuine and honest with yourself about who you are and what you want. It's about having substance and not a bunch of bells and whistles to cover up what may be lacking. Yes it's true, as I said many times, most men are initially drawn to what they see and this is usually a woman's physical attributes, but this is not what keeps a man for the long term. The fact is there are a lot of women that got it going on physically, but this is not what makes a woman necessarily special.

Contrary to what you might think, ladies... it's not the car you drive, the designer clothes you wear, or Barbie doll image that makes a man consider you special. It's that inner confidence to be yourself and know yourself. The ability to exude sexiness and classiness in your walk and the way you carry yourself. That sweet, kind and thoughtful personality and the ability to make a man feel like a man and not emasculate him. The intelligence to be his sounding board, the strength to support and encourage him, and the belief in your man. These things give a man something to really think about.

Don't you get it, ladies? IT'S ABOUT WHAT'S ON THE INSIDE that makes a man say WOW! What just happened? The substance... that inner quality you bring to the table makes a man think about and eventually want to settle down. Yes it's true, men are visual in that they are drawn to what they see from a physical standpoint, and no one is saying appearance doesn't matter when it comes to getting a man's attention. This is still very important in the grand scheme of things because you want a man to notice you first before he gets the know all of your other great attributes. But make no mistake about it, the way you look on the outside is not what will make a man want to take you home to meet his mother and ultimately put a ring on your finger.

Now how do you know if the man you're with loves you... and by this I mean good, healthy love? Not that obsessive, possessive or controlling type of distorted love. I mean you'll know when a man loves you by his actions, as I've said many times. A man who really has that good, healthy love for you will respect your thoughts, opinions and feelings. He will respect you enough to be on time when you plan a date. He will respect you enough to keep his word. He will be thoughtful in doing things for you just because. He will not play games to make you question is he keeping it real with you and does he really care about you. He will want to spend time with you, show you off to his friends and family, take you home to meet his mother. He will put your needs first—like giving you that last piece of cake so to speak. And most importantly, ladies, you will feel loved because of his actions. If you feel anything but that good, healthy love, you need to seriously decide—Do I want better? Because I know I deserve better.

Recap: Ladies...it's not what's on the outside that makes a man fall in love. It's what's on the inside. A woman will know when a man really loves her, not just by what he says, but more importantly by his actions.

CHAPTER 15

I Love My Man but I Don't Want To...

Ladies... let me start by saying that it's cool to love your man and to try to be "down" and please him. What is not cool is doing something you feel pressured to do or something you're truly uncomfortable with, even if it means disappointing someone you love. You should always be true to yourself.

That said... it's true that relationships are about compromise, but this should not be one sided. It is important for two people to respect each other's feeling in a relationship. For the purpose of this chapter, I want to focus on sexual exploration. The idea of sexual exploration in a relationship can be all good as long as you both agree on and are comfortable with whatever it is you are exploring.

Now I want to address you, ladies, because I think more often than men, you are the ones who are asked to step outside of your comfort zone—like not using protection or feeling pressured to do certain sexual acts. You fear that if you don't, you are not being "down," or your man will get upset and maybe even find someone else to do the things you won't do.

It may be true in some cases that a man will seek out another woman to do certain sexual things his woman won't do. But hear me, ladies, when I tell you that is his problem, not yours. That just means it was never really about you, it was his issue. You should not view yourself as inadequate as a woman just because you did not want to compromise who you are as a person.

You can live with a man walking out or stepping out, but if you give in, I can assure you will have regrets. And if a man cheats for this reason, he was not a "real" man to begin with for not respecting your feelings or understanding the woman you truly are. Moreover, if a man steps out with another woman for this reason, you can believe he was going to cheat anyway and was just looking for an excuse to justify his actions.

Again, ladies... you have to always respect yourself first before a man will respect you. A man will respect you more if you stay true to yourself... just keepin' it real. If he doesn't, you need to question whether he is really the right person for you. By not setting limits or staying true to yourself, you need to ask yourself the question—How far would I have to go to please my man?

What Does This Mean If I'm Married?

If you are married, there is no real difference in wanting to be respected although you love your husband. Yes relationships are about being able to compromise on things that both parties can see the benefit of, but not something that makes you feel bad or have regrets for doing. You should not feel pressured to do something you don't agree with or don't want to do, even if your husband is making the request.

If your husband claims that he really loves you, he will respect and understand how you feel. He will not make you feel pressured or guilty to do something you don't want to do out of a wifely obligation. You are still an individual first. Limits and boundaries should be respected even between husbands and wives.

What If My Man Wants to Bring a Third Party into Our Bedroom?

Again, ladies... if your man makes a request to bring a third party into your bedroom (woman or man... yeah I said another man... it happens), you still have to ultimately be comfortable with the request. Now a man requesting to bring another man into your bedroom can throw you for a loop... I'm sure! But serious talk, this is not a reflection on you in any way and it can happen to anybody.

Now for some of you, ladies, it may be easy to walk away from a man you've only been dating, but if you are married, it may not be so easy. If a man makes this type of request, I want to say this is not a common request for a man who claims to be heterosexual... again just keepin' it real.

A man, straight man that is, might fantasize or request to bring another woman into the bedroom but not another man. The fact is most men cannot even fathom the idea of their woman being with another man. I would be very curious about the suspicious nature of this request. Is he secretly bisexual or gay and is he afraid to come out of the closet? Maybe he is looking for a cover up to his friends and family. But whatever the underlining issue is, you have to communicate with him to try to uncover the truth and seek some type of counseling to help work through any issues you might have.

At the end of the day... bringing a third party, woman or man, into the bedroom is a VERY slippery slope. I call it opening Pandora's Box. It is an unpredictable situation even if you both set very clear grounds rules—such as this is only going to be a one-time deal or neither person can be with the third party alone. There is still no guarantee that the relationship will not fall apart. Essentially this can lead to jealousy, trust issues, or even violence (i.e., you seem to like the other person more than me, or you never made that sound or screamed that loud with me, or asking the question are you still seeing the other person behind my back). Even if this is only in his or her imagination and not the reality, it could definitely destroy the relationship. And once certain lines have been crossed, often times it is very hard to get back what you once had.

Recap: Love is about mutual respect, not about control.

CHAPTER 16

Reasons a Woman Might Feel Turned Off after Saying "I do"

Ladies... now that you said, "I do," are you feeling like your man is no longer communicating with you or being attentive to your needs? Are you feeling frustrated as hell? This can definitely have a direct impact on a woman feeling turned off after saying, "I do."

Well I get it, ladies... just because you said, "I do," doesn't mean that you want to stop feeling and being treated like a woman. This is what is called cultivating and nurturing a relationship like a delicate flower. And we all know what happens to a flower if you don't take care of it... it will wither and die. Well this is what happens sometimes after you say, "I do," because of variety of reasons. But it is not your responsibility alone to keep the relationship alive and thriving... it takes two to tango. But before we explore how you might be feeling, let's first look at how you got here...

I need to back it up first and ask a very important question... did you say, "I do," for all the **wrong** reasons? Think about it! Could it be that you settled for someone out of pressure from family and friends? Even the man who is now your husband would not stop pressuring you about marriage—he was constantly trying to put you on lock down and you felt obligated because of the time you spent together and had invested?

Maybe your girlfriends perceived your man as a great catch and would say things like, "Girl... why are you trippin'... if you don't want him, one of us will take him?" Or could it be that you said, "I do," because it just seemed like the right thing to do at the time. Maybe you said it because you were young, inexperienced, and he was all you'd ever known. Maybe you felt a sense of familiarity and got comfortable, or maybe you said, "I do," because you wanted to feel secure financially and he seemed like he would be a good provider. Maybe you said it because he was very handsome and charming, but he was never really that attentive to your needs because of his own narcissism. Or maybe he was just not who you expected to spend the rest of your life with but it just happened.

Well don't feel alone if you fit the bill for any of the examples I mentioned because you're not. These are very common reasons why some women say, "I do," and why you might be feeling turned off after marriage. What's important is that you recognize why you may be dissatisfied after marriage in order to do something about it. If this is the case, I will give you some possible things to consider that will hopefully help give you some direction.

Now if you said, "I do," for all the *right* reasons and you still feel turned off after marriage, here are some important questions that you need to ask yourself. Is he still the man he was when you first met? Are you the same woman? Do you feel as though you have grown apart? This is a common thing that can happen to some couples who have been together for a while.

Maybe you were young when you met and things are different now that you are older. Maybe you have different ideas about what you want out of life when it comes to creating a family, pursuing a career, or chasing your dreams. Maybe you have different interests or things that you want to explore or experience in life and your partner is just okay with status quo. This just does not excite you anymore and you are tired of the same ole same ole. Or maybe you are just feeling stymied or not able to grow because you are not feeling supported. Maybe the man you are with was once attentive and now he is neglecting you or taking you for granted. Maybe the sex isn't as intense or frequent as it used to be.

Just one little caveat, ladies, if sexual frequency and intensity is an issue, or lack thereof, this can happen for many reasons and it is important to really explore what the reasons are before you jump to any conclusions. I know a common conclusion for some women is that their man is probably seeing another woman. But this is not always the case. Relationships are about cycles, hot and cold spells, perhaps the timing never seems right. Maybe there is the responsibility of raising kids, or maybe there are new expectations or pressures at work. Maybe just being at a crossroad about one's plans for the future and life in general is taking a toll. While these issues should not be ongoing, these are valid issues that should be explored and hopefully worked through. But this will take some effort and commitment on both parts. Anything worth having is worth working hard to hang onto.

All of the things I mentioned have different meanings for different couples—some are big issues and some are small. Some are issues that can be managed and worked through to find a common solution with hard work and effort on both parts. And some are issues that cannot be just tolerated, managed, or expected to just work themselves out.

Ultimately, ladies, you have to decide how you feel in the relationship. You have to ask yourself are you happy or do you feel like that flower dying inside. Is your man still giving you all the love, encouragement, and support you need to continue to blossom and feel nurtured in the relationship? I don't just mean buying you diamonds and designer clothes and taking you on trips around the world. Although I get it... ain't nothing wrong with wanting some of those things, but this shouldn't take the place of having real substance in a relationship.

What I mean is support and nurture in the way of helping with the kids, helping with managing the bills, helping around the house, being attentive when you need his attention, being encouraging and a good listener when you need to feel supported, and of course romancing you when you need to be romanced. Are you still growing together and working together as a team? Are you still compatible in every way that makes you feel good inside? This is how you nurture and cultivate a relationship. And if you are no longer getting these things, ladies, again this could a big reason why you might be feeling turned off after marriage.

I'm a strong proponent of relationships, and I believe that if a couple can work it out, they should work it out in every possible way by communication or seeking out someone to offer them guidance (i.e., therapy or spiritual counseling or of course reading a self-help book like *Just Keepin' it Real, Ladies*).

On the other hand, I am not saying that you should stay in a relationship if you are feeling extremely unhappy or feeling the relationship is unhealthy. You have to decide. But while you are trying to figure it out and work it out, don't make the classic mistake of thinking that the grass will be greener on the other side. Again, this is a common mistake made by both men and women and will only compound the issue. For some reason, we believe that another person will not have the same character flaws that the person we're with has, or that we're getting the BBD (Bigger Better Deal). Sure, we might get that one thing that's missing from our man or woman. But let me tell if you "step out" for this reason, this is almost never the case. This is real talk! The other person may give you something the person you're with is missing, but more times than not you'll get a lot more than you bargained for. Everyone has character flaws because no one is perfect. And, ladies, don't think for one second that the other man is not thinking that if you stepped out on your man to be with him that you wouldn't do the same to him. You can never build a relationship on lies and deception.

The bottom line is, ladies, if you are feeling turned off after you said, "I do," and are making a choice when it comes to your relationship, the key essentials you should always use to help guide you are: Can I still communicate with my man at the end of the day? Do I still genuinely love this person? Do I genuinely like this person and vice versa, and do I genuinely feel good and happy MOST of the time when I'm with this person? And trust me when I tell you the rest will work itself out.

Recap: The words "I do" are simple words but have huge meaning. I believe most women have fantasized at one time or another about marrying their prince charming and living happily ever after. But often times this is not the case because it's not with the right guy or for the right reasons. Real talk! Ladies, don't get caught up in in trying to please others or trying to fit the wrong guy into your fantasy because you're growing impatient and want to be married. If it doesn't feel right, don't force it. Otherwise, you can find yourself feeling turned off after saying I do.

CHAPTER 17

What Are Some Things That Turn Men On and Off?

Well, ladies... if you were ever curious about things that turn men on and off... let me break it down for you. Just keep in mind that all men are not created the same and you still have to take the time to get to know what your man's specific likes and dislikes are. But I do think there are general things that men share in common about what turns them on and off. So first I'll start by telling you some of things that can be a turn off for men.

One-Night Stands

If you are surprised by one-night stands being a turn off, ladies, don't be. One-night stands are just what they are, one night. They are not called multiple-night stands for a reason. It is what it is. A one-night stand typically does not end up being a long-lasting relationship, and if it does develop into one, it is the exception to the rule.

That said... if given the opportunity to have sex with a woman who is "hot" on the first night, most men will not turn it down. As I said many times throughout this book, men are visual and physical in nature when it comes to women. Just keepin' it real... most men will not pump the breaks in the heat of the moment if the woman doesn't. If a man has the green light... trust me, he will go from zero to sixty in a second trying to get the Cali Poppy.

Although a one-night stand does not always equate to a man being turned off, I would say it definitely sends the wrong message initially. The message it sends is that the woman is easy, does not have a lot of respect for herself, and probably sleeps around, even if this is not necessarily the case. I know this seems like a double standard and men should be judged by the same standard as women, but in reality men are not.

The good news is not all men think this way, but the bad news is I would say that it is probably the shared notion of a lot of men. And it is probably not the best way to start out if you are looking for a long-term relationship. There is a lot of truth to first impressions. The truth is most men want a woman to play a little hard to get even if the chemistry and sexual attraction is crazy off the hook. I said this before but I think it's important to reiterate, "The fruit that is farther from the tree is better than the fruit that falls at your feet." Nobody wants something that is too easy to get or something used up, even if this is only the perception. What is harder to get is more desirable and you're more likely to cherish it when you get it.

So, ladies, if you can avoid a one-night stand, it is probably a good idea to do so. However, if you do decide to have a one-night stand... it's important to use very good judgment in selecting the guy and let your instincts guide you... hopefully this will be enough. If this is the case, I would say do not go into it with any expectations. You may be disappointed if you realize you really like a guy and he does not reciprocate your feelings because you sent the wrong message from the start.

Remember, ladies, men in general want a woman they can respect and feel proud of.

Drama/Bad attitude

If a woman constantly has a negative attitude or is creating drama, this can be another turn off. Most men would likely agree that next to good sex is having a home that is drama free. Before you go there, ladies, and start rolling your eyes, snapping your fingers and saying, "No he didn't..." let me clarify. I'm talking about a situation where a woman has a negative attitude or is creating drama when unprovoked.

Yes... it's true...some men incite drama or bring out the worse in women by doing foolish things—not communicating, lying, being lazy, and even disrespecting their woman or taking her for granted. I get it, ladies, and I understand if you have a bad attitude for any of these reasons, rightfully so. I'm talking about when a man is trying to do the right things like working hard, being faithful, providing a nice home, and catering to most or all of your needs but it is still not enough. He is still constantly nagged about where he's going, who is he with, or why didn't he do X, Y & Z.

Men do not handle drama well and the more drama in the home, the more a man will seek out an environment that is perceived to be drama free. I think it is important to appreciate your man for the positives, especially if they far outweigh the negatives. Yes, this goes both ways, ladies. I also believe that there is a good way to communicate effectively with your man, and a not-so-good way. The not so good way is using a tone that seems accusatory, demeaning, emasculating, dictating, or controlling. Negative communication is just not the way to go and will not get you what you want. Also remember timing is very important when communicating with a man.

Too Emotionally Needy or Clingy

Being too emotionally needy or clingy can also be a big turn off to men. Most men do not do well when it comes to handling a woman who is too emotionally needy or clingy. Men do not typically do well expressing their feelings much less having to deal with a woman who can't control her feelings and is needing constant reassurance. Examples are constantly asking her man to tell her that she is beautiful or wanting him to constantly tell her how much he loves her.

While this is natural to want once in a while, there is such a thing as overkill, ladies, in wanting a man to constantly express his undying feelings and love for you. Unfortunately a lot of men do not communicate this way, but this does not mean he doesn't love you or think you're beautiful. Hopefully the man is expressing his love and feelings for you in the most important way and that is by his actions.

Another classic example of being needy or clingy is a woman wanting to spend all of her time with her man. Ladies... let's be real... there are only twenty-four hours in a day and sometimes this is still not enough time to fully satisfy a woman's need to spend time with a man she really likes. You've got to let a man breathe and not smother him.

Do not make the classic mistake and chase a good man away by being too clingy or needy, no matter how much you like him or perceive he is Mr. Right. If you meet a guy who has "potential," there is probably a fear that someone else will snag him from under you or he will lose interest if you are not spending all of your time with him. But that's not the case. You have to show some restraint even if you are really diggin' a guy.

I can't emphasize this enough, especially when you first meet a guy. Men like a challenge and playing a little cat mouse in the beginning is okay. This gets a guy thinking about the type of woman you are...it piques his curiosity about you. If you come on too strongly right away, a man will think you require more attention than he is willing to give and he can see this only getting worse as time goes on. This is especially common after sex.

As I said before, women tend to get more emotionally attached after sexual intimacy. Men, on the other hand, can generally detach more easily than women. The trick is, ladies, you have to be more like men in this case. My suggestion is whatever you had going on before you met the guy (i.e., being independent, hobbies, spending time with friends and family) you should continue to maintain this. If the relationship develops and progresses into to more, and spending more time with each other is mutual, then let it flow naturally.

Too Controlling

Let me tell you, ladies... no man really likes to be controlled and this can be a major turn off. This is a mistake that many women make and they end up chasing a good man away. You know what I'm talking about, ladies... doing things for a man that he can do for himself—telling your man what clothes to wear, how to fix his hair, giving him a curfew, telling him who he can and can't hang out with.

Some women go as far as to try and control what goes on in the bedroom. I have even heard that some women give their men a "honey do" list... you know, honey do this, and honey do that. Women wonder why some men view marriage as serving hard time. Well look no further if this is your Modus Operandi, ladies.

Let me tell you, controlling or emasculating a man may not stop you from getting that ring, but it will definitely keep that man from wanting to come home at night. This is part of the reason why some men act out and go to strip clubs and bars. Many of them feel they need some type of outlet or escape from the control they are experiencing at home. If you really want your man to buy in to what you're selling, so to speak, without him feeling like you're are trying to control him, you might try giving him praise and encouragement when he does something well or something you like. This will motivate him to want to repeat the same things.

If he does something you don't like, there is nothing wrong with being honest and direct with him in a nice way about what you don't like. But because men have egos, it's always good to preface whatever it is that you don't like with saying something good about him first. For example, "I love you, babe, for who you are and I'm not trying to change you, but can I make a suggestion..." This makes it easier for a man to accept your constructive criticism and not view it as negative. And, ladies, if a man can do for himself, let him. There is a difference between doing a nice gesture occasionally for your man and doing everything for him. The worst thing you can do is have a grown man become dependent on you.

Essentially, ladies, men like to feel like they are kings of their castles and not feel like they are on lock down. You don't want your man marking the days on the calendar like he is incarcerated and counting down until he gets released.

High Maintenance

A woman being too high maintenance is a very big turn off to most men. A man will view a woman as high maintenance if she always seems to require an abundance of attention or things to please her. This type of woman cannot be satisfied with anything that seems average, ordinary or simple.

A high-maintenance woman may be categorized as always NEEDING to have her hair or nails done at the beauty shop no matter the cost or who pays for it. She always has to have the most expensive or trendy clothes, she always wants to dine at the finest restaurants, or she always has to be driving the nicest car.

This type of woman thinks a guy is cheap if he is not taking her on trips, shopping sprees, or wining and dining her every week. Plain and simple, she has to have what she wants when she wants it. A high-maintenance woman might also be perceived as never being appreciative. Whatever a man does for her is never enough.

While some men might deal with a high maintenance woman (usually because she looks good... just keepin' it real), most men will shy away from this type of woman. Even if a man can afford to buy this type of woman anything she wants, he will ultimately be turned off by her attitude, lack of appreciation, and the feeling that he's being used.

Now, ladies, I'm not knocking a woman who is independent and can do all the things she wants for herself. This is a sexy quality to have. And I'm not saying that a woman should not want nice things or want to be catered to once in a while, but being high maintenance is an issue when the standards are too high, too superficial, and you **EXPECT** to have everything your way all the time (Like Burger King, always gotta have it your way). It is also an issue if things are always about you but never appreciated or reciprocated. The pressure and expectation of a high-maintenance woman can prove to be too much trouble and work for any man to want to deal with.

Conceited/Stuck up

A woman who is stuck up or conceited is definitely a huge turn off, but this should come as no real surprise. You think? Well...you'd be surprised to know there are still a lot of women that fit this mold and do not get it because they are too self-absorbed. This type of woman has her head so far in the clouds she can't see anyone. She will look right past a guy or through him like he was never standing there. This type of woman carries herself as though she's beyond approach and then wonders why she can never find a good man.

Well first, a man cannot even get close to this type of woman unless she deems him worthy. And a guy's worthiness in her eyes is usually someone who can match her in beauty or someone she sees as having lots of money or status... again just keepin' it real. If she is beautiful likes she thinks, some guys will tolerate this type of woman and probably give her everything she wants, but it will all be based on superficial qualities.

This type of woman will use a guy for whatever he can give her and he in turn uses her for what she can give him, which is usually sex. But most men will not deal with this type of woman. In fact, most men will view this type of woman as unattractive because of how she is on the inside, even if she is stunningly beautiful on the outside. And also keep in mind, ladies, that a flower is not always in bloom. Physical beauty fades, but what's on the inside is something that lasts a lifetime.

Having Too Much Baggage Can Be another Turn Off for Men

If a woman has too many past relationships, this can sometimes be considered a turn off, although not always. If she has too much "baggage," she may be viewed as possibly having skeletons in the closet, or maybe still having some attachment to one or more of her exes, especially if there are children involved. In other words, depending on whether any of her past relationships were long-term or significant, a woman may still be connected to an ex, either financially or by residual feelings for that man, depending on how the relationship ended.

It may take longer for a woman to sever that relationship or move on if she really loved her ex. Some men don't want to compete with a woman's lingering affections for an ex. And if the ex is still in the picture, say because of children, even if the woman no longer loves him, the new man might have to deal with possible jealousy issues on the part of the ex if the split wasn't mutual. The ex might feel a sense of rights or entitlement to the woman, especially if there are children involved. This might be more than the new man is willing to deal with. Another major problem with an ex is that the relationship, if a bad one, might have caused that woman to feel slighted or jaded when it comes to forming a new relationship. She might be dealing with trust issues if she's been burned in the past, and she might take these insecurities out on the new guy. He then becomes everything negative that she experienced in her previous relationship(s) and she recreates the drama in the new relationship. This is just something to be aware of, ladies, in terms of how some men (but not all) might view a woman's past relationships.

What Are Some Things That Might Turn a Man On?

Big Butt

If a woman has a big booty, junk in the trunk, apple bottom, gluteus maximus, badonkadonk, or onion booty (the booty is so big...it makes you want to cry), this can be a huge turn on for a man. A big butt used to be viewed more as an asset in certain cultures, particularly in the African American and Latin culture. However, nowadays a big butt seems to be a growing trend among all women, and men everywhere are admiring a woman with a big butt.

The male's attraction to a woman with a big butt is causing women to do all sorts of things to get it. Women are doing all kinds of butt crunches, buying butt underwear, getting butt lifts and even buying artificial implants. If a woman has a big butt, this is considered a nice asset or physical feature that many men will be drawn to. Men have gotten whiplash and eyes have literally bulged out of their sockets over a woman with a big butt. As I've said many times, men are visual and physical in nature, and a woman having a big butt is a nice feature that many men like for their viewing pleasure.

Breasts

Breasts are another great physical feature, like the butt. Unlike having a big butt, women with nice breasts have not been exclusive to certain cultures. This is a common asset that is shared by women of all races. This is another physical feature that women possess and men go absolutely crazy over. The benefits of having nice breasts are no secret to women. That's why some women go to great lengths to enhance what they have.

Very much like the butt, women do breast exercises to firm up their breasts, wear push up bras, and even get implants to enhance their physical appearance and look. While I believe women enhance their breasts to feel good about themselves, they also do it to attract men's attention... let's be real.

Because men are visual and enjoy admiring the female anatomy, women with nice breasts tend to get a lot of attention and perks. And while a big butt and breasts are very nice features for a woman to have, they can be both assets and curses for a woman because sometimes that's all some men see.

I would caution, ladies, that if these types of physical qualities are all you bring to the table, they will certainly be enough to get a man but not enough to keep him. And you don't want to be defined only by what's on the outside. Plenty of women can be admired for their physical beauty, but a woman with substance is a rarity. These types of women tend to have greater success when it comes to sustaining a relationship or being viewed as marriage material. For men, the body catches our eye, but what's inside captures our hearts.

Pretty Eyes

There is something about a woman with pretty eyes that captivates and can command a man's attention. Pretty eyes are a single feature, like the butt and breasts, that can actually stand alone in attracting a man's attention. A woman with pretty eyes can be viewed as memorizing, alluring and seductive.

Beautiful Smile and Nice Lips

A beautiful smile and nice lips are features that can be a turn on for men much like pretty eyes. While pretty eyes might have a slight advantage because they carry a certain mystic and seductiveness that men love, a beautiful smile is quite attractive and a turn on for men as well. Men love a woman with a beautiful smile because it can mean that a woman is not mad at the world. Although a beautiful smile can sometimes be deceiving, it can also mean that a woman has a beautiful disposition.

Men are definitely drawn to women with a beautiful smile. If a woman has nice lips, this is an added bonus...usually nice lips are an alluring quality to men because of the kissable element. The perception is—if a woman has nice lips, she is probably a good kisser and can please a man in other ways as well. Women are also getting enhancements in their lips to make them fuller. Larger lips were not always viewed as a beautiful feature to have. So, ladies, if you have larger, fuller lips, you should definitely be proud of this quality and embrace it.

Hair

Hair is another important feature on a woman and it will definitely get a man's attention if a woman takes pride in her hair. Although hair is probably is a little further down on the hierarchy list of what turns men on, it is still considered an attractive feature because a man generally notices a woman's hair at same time he notices that she is attractive.

If a woman is attractive but her hair is not properly maintained, this could definitely be a turn off. This is one of the reasons women spend hundreds of dollars keeping their hair right and tight. The problem is some women think that they are too cute to get her hair a little messed up. You feel what I'm saying, ladies...you can't have a strand of hair out place, don't want anybody touching your hair, and God forbid getting a drop of water on it...you would think that you were going to melt like the Wicked Witch of the West from *The Wizard of Oz*.

Trust me, ladies. I get it. It costs money and time to get your hair done, and when you get it just right you don't want anybody or anything messing it up. Hair can also mean different things for different women culturally. But this goes back to what I mentioned earlier about a woman being too high maintenance or too focused on her outer beauty.

Ladies, men don't want a woman who cares more about her hair than she cares about having a good time. It's okay to let your hair down on occasions and have a good time. A sexy quality is when a woman is real (above the image) and is not OVERLY focused on how she looks, including her hair.

I also want to mention that hair does not necessarily have to be long for a man to be turned on by your look. It can be short as well. And it's not necessarily about "good" hair or "bad" hair or hair that is "real" or "fake." The fact is different guys have different preferences, so don't stress about it. If a woman takes pride in her hair, no matter what she working with, and she has self-confidence, this will certainly attract a man's attention. And if a guy is not diggin' you for how you wear your hair—the texture, or length—you should keep it movin' because that is his loss.

Nice Legs and Pretty Feet

A great pair of legs on a woman can be extremely sexy, simply put. A woman with nice feet is also very attractive and a turn on, but, ladies you have to keep your feet on point. If your feet always look like you've been walking on the beach or your shoes have lumps indented in them from bunions, this can definitely be a turn off. And, ladies, please chill on wearing the open toe shoes if your feet aren't right. Bad feet on a woman are definitely not attractive. This might make a man question how a woman could have it going on everywhere else and not take care of her feet. I'm just saying...

Intelligence

Ladies, don't think men don't recognize or appreciate a woman with a brilliant mind because they do. This is another big turn on for men. It may not be at the top of the list in terms of importance initially because of a man's physical nature, but a woman who is beautiful and has a mind is the ultimate complete package. Plenty of men find intelligent, smart witted women stimulating and sexy.

However, I would be remiss if I didn't mention that there are also men who are intimidated by intelligent women. But usually these types of guys have not reached a level of maturity to relate or appreciate a woman with this great quality. There are probably some insecurity issues on his part as well. And there are some guys who perceive a smart woman as a challenge because she is not easily manipulated (i.e., easy to get the sex, won't question suspicious behavior, etc.).

On the flip side, some women are too smart for their own good and use their intelligence to one up a man by putting him down or being argumentative just for the sake of being argumentative or right. This is a definite turn off and a big complaint of a lot of men. Relationships should not be about competition or who is always right or smarter than the other person. It's about being able to compromise no matter who's right or wrong.

Secure

If a woman is secure with herself, this is definitely a big turn on and a sexy quality to say the least. Most men revere women who are secure because these women know exactly who they are as a person and what they want in life. A secure woman is above playing a lot of games with a man to get his attention. She believes in a man accepting her for who she is. This type of woman doesn't derive confidence from a man because her confidence comes from within. She knows how to compliment a man but is not defined by a man. But most importantly, a secure woman loves and respects herself above all else.

Nice Personality

Now last, but definitely not least, a huge turn on for men is a woman with a nice personality. This includes, but is not limited to, her sense of humor, kindness, thoughtfulness, compassion, support, dependability, trust, strength, and most importantly self-respect. I would be lying if I said that personality is the first thing a man looks for in a woman, but as I said many times, men are drawn to what they see.

However, the way a woman looks on the outside can only go so far if she does not have a great personality to go along with it. The truth is—if a woman has a great personality, this is what not only gets a man's attention. It's what keeps it. A man is more likely to respect a woman with a beautiful personality and is less likely to want to hurt her or take advantage of her.

On the other hand, if a woman has a not-so-attractive personality or disposition, a man might not feel as remorseful if he treats her bad...just keepin' it real. A nice personality separates a woman from all the rest. As I said before, outer beauty is not a rare quality to find... think about it... I'm sure you know of beautiful women (even Celebs) who've been cheated on or ended up divorced. This is not to say that they had bad personalities, but if it was about their external beauty, this would not be the case. A woman with a beautiful personality is like a rare precious jewel that is very much desired and sought after. You certainly can't find it all the time. And if the right person finds this rare jewel, he will definitely cherish it. The key word is the RIGHT person!

Bottom line is... a lot of things turn men on and off. And as mentioned, a lot of those things that turn men on happen to be the physical attributes of a woman. This is just keeping one hundred percent real with you, ladies. Most men are turned on by what they see. But the point I want to make clear is that what turns men on is not necessarily what makes them stick, especially if all you have to offer is physical.

The inner qualities of a woman not only turn a man on but keep him turned on for the long-term. I also want to reiterate that I have given you some general or common things that turn men off and on, but you still have to find out what makes your man tick as all men are not created the same.

Recap: As talked about in this chapter, many things turn men on and off—whether the character of a woman or her physical attributes. But, ladies... if all you have to offer is your physical attributes, this might turn a man on but will not make him stick. And you don't want to be valued or defined by how you look because that is temporary and conditional. What is more valuable and will stand the test of time is having great inner qualities. And, ladies... know that whatever you bring to the table as far as physical appearance is good enough for any man. If he cannot appreciate you for how you look, that is his problem and his loss. Trust me, there are plenty of men that will.

CHAPTER 18

Why Do Some Men Change after Getting the Cali Poppy (Sex)?

Ladies...let me see if I understand the question. You want to know why in the beginning he seemed attentive, laughed at all your jokes, told you how beautiful you were constantly, seemed to listen to all your problems, and then you gave up the Cali Poppy and he changed? Hmm... well, while there is no single answer to this question, I will give you some possible reasons a man might seem to treat you differently after sex. It takes to two to tango, so keep that in mind as I attempt to answer this question. You also have to consider what part you played in his change after sex. And I will explain what I mean by that.

First of all, I want to let you know, ladies, that sex will definitely get you a man, but it will not guarantee you will keep that man. Real talk...

Second, ladies, men don't really change after sex per se. If a man seems to have changed after sex, I can assure you he was never really true to it anyway. What I mean by this is that he was fronting and faking with you about what you meant to him from the get go. Just keepin' it real... there were probably obvious signs that you noticed. Things didn't seem right in his stories and behavior, little inconsistencies, and you just chose to ignore the signs.

Now I'm not condoning a man's behavior or blaming the victim, but you've got to keep it real with yourself on the part you played in letting him play you. Some guys have some real character flaws (i.e., conceit, deceit, obsessive, possessive, and controlling). If you still chose to have sex with a guy who fit any of these criteria, and there were obvious signs, then it should not be all that surprising when a guy seems to change after sex.

If he is controlling, he just becomes more controlling. If he is deceitful or a "dog" he just becomes more of a dog. And, ladies, you've got to stop making excuses, rationalizing, or trying to justify a man's behavior or actions. Accept the fact that a lot of times, it is what it is. Don't IGNORE the signs!

Ladies, you've also got to ask questions, and more questions, and more questions. A lot of guys just want the sex and nothing more. So you have to keep it real with yourself when you meet a guy about your expectations. The truth is—if you don't know what you want or expect coming into the sexual relationship, it's fair game. Basically, you are just going with the flow and whatever happens, happens. You can't be surprised if a guy does not want what you want or he wants to do something else after sex.

The fact is you did not let him know that you were looking for something more serious or long-term, so the guy is really under no obligation to be real with you or keep what you think you have going. You have to know what you want and then communicate this to the guy when you meet him. If he deceives you after you have been honest with him, that is his issue and you can't be responsible for his actions.

Lastly... ladies, you also have to be real with yourself about the part you played in a man seeming to change after sex. Was it really him who changed or was it you? Did you flip the script? Did you have your own agenda or secret expectations going into the sexual relationship but they were not communicated to the guy. Did you decide that he was potentially a good catch because he looked good, had a nice car, had money, or said all the right things? And you got caught in the fantasy of making him your man. This is giving some women the benefit of the doubt because some men don't even have to fit these criteria to be a considered a good catch.

Some men are just plain broken down and this will not stop some women from wanting to be with them... sorry, I digress. But, ladies, seriously, if a guy is clearly sending you signals or saying that he is not available or does not want a committed relationship, you cannot change the game after sex. You cannot be demanding all of his time, expecting him to spend more time with you, calling him 24/7, or getting upset if he does not call you back right away, or at all. Again he is under no obligation or contractual agreement to do or be anything more because you chose to give him the sex.

A lot of times, ladies, your actions after sex change the dynamics and this seems as though the man has changed. Some women become very clingy, dependent, possessive, obsessive, and so forth. Usually this is because the woman is now very emotionally attached. The problem is putting it on too thick in the beginning will usually back fire.

So, ladies, limit the calls (one call is sufficient) and allow him to return your call or let him make the first move. Don't be too available or accessible after sex (he might see this as being too desperate) and don't come across as a stalker... Showing up at his job or home with cupcakes uninvited, especially if he didn't give you the address, will definitely cause him to think you are crazy as hell.

I say keep it simple, ladies... be honest with yourself and the guy about what you want and the expectations before sex. If you don't set ground rules going in from the start, whatever happens, happens and you can't get upset later or flip the script expecting more. Also, you have to stop ignoring the obvious signs or making excuses for a guy's character flaws... it is what it is and usually a guy will not change just because you think you put it on him or somehow you think you are different than the last woman he was with.

On the other hand, if you keep it simple and straight forward about what you want and expect from a guy, you lower your chances of getting hurt or a guy seeming to change after sex because you are not putting yourself in that position. In other words, a lot of guys who just want the sex don't really want to put in a lot of work to get it. If you express your wants and expectations up front... this will sound like too much work for some guys. By this alone you're able to weed out some of the guys who just have one intention... sex. And, contrary to popular belief, some men actually have a conscience that will not allow them to take advantage of a woman if they know her expectations. Also, by letting a guy know what you want or expect, you are sending the message to him that the sex with you is not free... you expect some level of commitment and respect.

It's true that some guys will put in whatever work they need to deceive you (to get the sex) and say and do all the right things, but you have to see the signs, the character flaws, and then keep it moving.

Recap: I believe that when two people lay down, somebody will walk away with feelings. And in some cases, it could both the man and the woman who will catch feelings. But men have an easier time detaching emotionally, and sex for them can be purely physical. So often times the woman, more so than the man, will become more emotionally attached after sex. And when this happens, the woman starts to change because she wants to spend more time with the guy (naturally of course). But if he doesn't reciprocate those feelings, it appears as though he has changed. This is a typical scenario if it was just sex for the guy and no real or clear understanding of a commitment. That's why, ladies, it's always good to be very clear about what you want and expect from a man and know what his intentions are before you give up the Cali Poppy.

CHAPTER 19

A Woman Who Stands Out from the Crowd

This is real talk, ladies... if you really want to stand out from the crowd, I want you to really think about what I'm saying. Let me first start by saying it's not about the sex because a man can always get that. You can even look like Halle and have a body like Beyoncé, but it is still not enough. You can have a platinum card, drive a nice car, and be a lingerie type of lady, but it's not about that. What makes a woman stand out from the crowd is being confident but not cocky or conceited. If a woman is confident, this will grab a man's attention for sure.

A woman who exudes confidence usually feels good about herself and does not need a man to define her. This is not to say this type woman does not want a man in her life... it just means she feels good about herself even if she doesn't currently have a man. She will wait patiently until the right one comes along who will love and treat her the way she wants to be treated. This type of woman is also not trying to possess a man because she is secure with herself.

A woman who stands out from the crowd is not fake, phony or pretentious. She doesn't feel like she has to put on airs to please others or try to attract the attention of a man. She is merely comfortable with just being herself.

A woman who stands out from the crowd is an independent woman who can take care of herself. She does not need a man to provide for her financially or believe in using a man for what she can gain from him. However, this type of woman will accept a man doing for her if his intentions are good and honorable. She is not above reciprocity and doing nice or thoughtful gestures for a man in return if she cares about him.

A woman who stands out from the crowd is very modest about her outer beauty, but she is fully aware that true beauty comes from within. She does not have to get glammed up or have her hair perfectly styled all the time... she is very comfortable with sporting a ponytail or baseball cap if the occasion calls for it.

A woman who stands out from the crowd respects herself. Because she respects herself and carries herself this way, men will always respect her. This type of woman understands her self-worth and value. She carries herself with class and sophistication. She understands that she does not have to dress scantily or trashy to get a man's attention. This type of woman knows how to work what she is born with but understands that what she wears and how she carries herself is how she will be perceived by others (especially men). She is careful about sending the wrong message.

Bottom line, ladies, is... to stand out from the crowd, you have to be true to who you are. It's not about trying to please others or being something you're not. It's about loving and accepting yourself no matter what anyone thinks. You have to trust and believe that you are beautiful just the way you are. You attract what you put out there. And finally, it's about your mind and what's in your heart that really makes you stand out from the crowd.

Recap: Always be true to yourself, ladies. A real man will recognize how special you are.

CHAPTER 20

Can a Man Change His Ways?

First off, I think women are remarkable creations and not a lot of things can compare. Yeah, you got it going on, ladies... BUT... I have to say that some of you do way too much when it comes to a man. What I mean is that you're always looking for that silver lining or cup is half-full in a man. Basically, a lot of times you give a man too much benefit of the doubt when there is a whole lot of reason to doubt. Of course this does not apply to all women, but there are a lot of women that get the concept of "can a man change his ways" twisted. So I want to make this perfectly clear and point out some key factors with this concept.

Essentially, there are women who get a man and it turns out he is not everything they imagined him to be. They have a hard time accepting this reality or letting the relationship go. Sound familiar? These women, for various reasons, feel they might be letting their man down if they give up on him. They may feel a sense of duty to pick their man up and dust him off and make him the man they imagined. They may consider themselves a "ride or die" chic and want to have their man's back until the end.

They do all these things despite a man's infidelity, neglect, disrespect, immaturity, irresponsibility, "mama's boy" syndrome, or inability to commit. Like I said, ladies, way too much! Now, no offense, but a psychologist might say the reason some women will hang onto a man despite these major personality and character flaws is they are afraid to be alone, or desperate, or they have low self-esteem, or just in denial about the fact that their man is just plain ole no good or good for nothing. But whatever the reason, you have to start seeing and accepting things for what they are and not what you want them to be.

Look, it's simple... first you have to understand that it's not about trying to change a man, it is about changing how you see yourself in relation to a man. You have to love yourself first, second, and always, and know that a man does not define you. You have to stop trying to change a man because you can't... this is real talk.

No matter how much you are trying to be down for your man, no matter how you feel that he will somehow change if you just hang in there a little while longer, and no matter how much you think if you change something about yourself, he will change—these things WILL NOT change a man. The fact is if a man truly wants to change, he has to change himself. You have to either accept a man the way he is (the good, the bad or ugly) or keep it movin'. It's just that simple. It is not your job or responsibility to a change a man no matter how much you think you love or care about him. You just have to know what is healthy and good for you. AND NOT ALL MEN ARE GOOD FOR YOU ... AND THAT'S REAL TALK!

That said, you have to ultimately decide if the man you are with is capable of changing his ways. No one can decide this for you. I know some women will, despite what I've said, keep trying to change their man and will continue hanging on to their man no matter what. Because the truth is—matters of the heart do not always make sense, nor can they be explained logically. But know this... the definition of insanity is when you keep doing the same thing and expecting a different result.

However, if you are really trying to assess whether your man is capable of change, you don't have to look anything further than his behavior and actions. A man can tell you all he wants that he will change or has changed (and trust me, he will) but this does not mean anything unless he backs it up with action.

The real question is how long will it take you to see what is real. Not what your girlfriends or family have told you about your man but what you've seen with your own eyes. And please, ladies, keep it real with yourself about this change. Too often women make excuses about what is not real because they want to convince themselves or others in believing that their man has changed. And for those women who feel that they can't get anything better than what they already have, let me tell you, ladies, there are an estimated seven billion people in this world. Out of those seven billion people, at least half are men. So I ask the question, ladies...really? Do you really have to ask the question can a man change with those statistics? Don't ever limit yourself to just one guy or feel that you have to put up with a man if he's not treating you right. Like Beyoncé said, "I can have another you in a minute." Well you don't have to be Beyoncé to believe this ...with those statistics you can too and that's the attitude you have to have. This is real talk!

Recap: Ladies, don't try to change a man because you can't. He has to want to change. And it's not about whether or not a man can change his ways, what's important is that you believe you deserve a good man who will treat you the way you want and need to be treated.

CHAPTER 21

The Misperception of a Bad Boy/Thug

If I had dollar for every time I heard women say they can't find a good man... well, put it like this, I would be paid! And for the ones I've asked the question, "Why do you think you can't find a good man?" The answer is usually, "I'm not sure if a good man really exists."

When I ask them why they believe a good man does not exist, what I've found is they have been chasing this perception of a fantasy type of guy... what I call a misperception of a "bad boy" or "thug." I call it a misperception because I think, surprisingly, a lot of women have a false perception of what they think a bad boy or thug really is. Because of this, often times a good man is shunned or cast aside for this so-called bad boy or thug type. I want to talk about why some women have this misperception.

Now just keepin' it real, ladies, I don't believe you will find real love with a bad boy or thug, but I get why some women think that it is possible. Let me explain what I mean... I think a lot of women have this perception of a perfectly refined bad boy or thug. Before I expound on what I mean by a perfectly refined bad boy or thug, I think women (not all) have found themselves at some point or another drawn to that quasi-bad boy or villain type of guy in the movies with the pretty boy face that seems mysterious or just misunderstood.

The guy is usually portrayed as street smart and tough and just needs a good woman to understand him and help him see the light. And of course this guy turns out to be the hero in the movie and he and the woman live happily ever after... that is at least until the credits end.

Taking that guy I described off the big screen, women have created an all new and improved fantasy version bad boy or thug. This guy has all the GOOD characteristics that women are looking for in a man. He is the perfectly refined bad boy or thug. He is sexy, good looking, mysterious, adventurous, and has plenty of swag. He is tough and will fight for his lady's honor. He is a take-control type of guy who knows exactly what he wants and goes after it. He is someone who cleans up nicely in three-piece suit and can handle himself well in a boardroom. He is someone who comes home from work, changes into a tank top and shorts, puts on a hat to the back or slightly cocked the side, displaying a chiseled body. He then puts on Jay Z or R & B for background music, depending on the mood while his lady prepares dinner. He may offer to help cook dinner while asking his lady how her day went. And lastly, he will top off the day by pouring his lady a glass of Moscat and take her to the bedroom and put it on her... you know that leg shakin', hair all over place, where am I and how did I get here type of love making. Did I get it right, ladies?

Well, ladies... I get the fantasy of wanting to create the perfect man, but what I don't get is some women wanting to call this man a bad boy or thug. This is the big misperception. A "real" bad boy or thug is nothing like what you see on TV, the movies, or any fantasy you can dream up. There is a reason why bad boy has the word "bad" in it, and I don't care how you try to redefine thug it still has a negative connotation.

Even the late great Tupac, who popularized the term "Thug Life," defined thug as someone who is going through struggles, has gone through struggles, and continues to live day by day with nothing for them. A thug is not the imitator that comes from a suburban background and thinks a couple of tattoos, hat cocked to the side and saggin' pants makes him a thug. He is a different breed than your average guy because he is greatly influenced by the street life in which he grows up in.

Real thugs are typically hustlers or have a criminal mentality because they have to make a living any way they know how. They have a hard edge because you can't be soft or show weakness in the streets. They usually have little education (not to be confused with street smarts) because school is not a top priority for them. It's about survival.

They also struggle with trust issues because often they do not know who to trust and are constantly looking over their shoulder. So break that down, ladies. You're dealing with a guy who might have trust or commitment issues, may not have a legitimate job, may have a tough time communicating or expressing himself because of little or no education, and may be too hard to show a softer side when needed in terms of warmth and sensitivity. It is not entirely his fault that he is how he is. He is just the product of the environment in which he grew up. And as far as a bad boy goes, it should be pretty self-explanatory. It is no secret that bad boys struggle with trust and commitment issues. So in either case, ladies, is this someone you think you could really build a relationship with?

I get that there might be some things that seem intriguing, interesting or exciting about the movie or fantasy version bad boy or thug, which may have some elements of reality. But, ladies, you cannot ignore the real things that make them what they are. On the other hand, I believe that some men can learn some things that might serve them well from the fantasy or movie version bad boy or thug as crazy as that might sound.

Some of the qualities are being more assertive, standing strong and tall, being decisive and knowing how to take charge when needed, and walking with a certain outward confidence or swag. Others might include being a little less predictable to keep their woman guessing and not become boring, changing it up in the bedroom by making love with a certain animal-like passion and intensity, depending on what the mood dictates, and loosening up with annunciating every word like a Webster's dictionary. In other words, there is a time and place for everything. It's about being versatile, fellas, if you want women to stop chasing this fantasy type of guy and be perfectly satisfied with you... the reality. I'm just keepin' it real. Be smart, ladies...

Recap: Ladies... good men are out there who will respect you and treat you right. They even have a swag about them. You don't have to go looking for a bad boy or thug because trust me it will be more than you bargained for. And be careful about chasing a good man away because you think you want a so-called bad boy or thug because you might miss out on a good thing and find yourself unhappy and alone. And that's if you're lucky.

CHAPTER 22

Looking for a Man with the Big "P"

Ladies...if you've never heard of the "P" term, you are probably wondering what I mean by this. Well the big P is basically what a lot women look for in a man. And I don't mean that certain part of a man's anatomy below the waist...Mm hmm... I know what you were thinking. And I don't mean the fat pocket book either, although you probably wouldn't mind a man who has these things too.

What I mean by the big "P" is a man who has big potential. The truth is I think we all look for a person to complement us or bring something to the table that we can build a relationship on. There is nothing wrong with that, in fact, this is a great thing. I've said this many times throughout this book that, ladies, you should have some idea of the kind of man you want. This starts with having standards or certain qualities you look for in a man that you can work with. These qualities can signify a man's potential. And while having potential is certainly a good thing, it can also sometimes be misleading if you read too deeply into it, which I will explain later on.

Now what is potential? Potential can be defined as a person (man or woman) having certain abilities or qualities that MAY be developed and lead to future success or usefulness. In other words, if a man says a woman has potential to be the "ONE," this means he obviously sees certain qualities in that woman he really likes. He wants to see whether the relationship will continue to develop based on these qualities. Women are not that much different than men in this way except maybe a lot faster in deducing whether a man has potential or not.

You know what I'm talking about, ladies … a woman will see a man and immediately size him up in thirty seconds and determine whether he has potential. If a man appears attractive, nicely dressed, or walks with a certain confidence, immediately a woman's mind goes to work. She starts to process these things and right off the bat will make a determination of whether she can work with the guy based on what she sees as potential. For some women, first sight is just the beginning of her mission to find out if a guy has potential.

She may ask questions to find out things like whether he's educated, does he have children, does he have good credit, and does he have a good job. Some women even go as far as doing internet searches among other things to see what they can find out about a guy like is he married or does he have a criminal record. Am I right, ladies? Because generally women are sizing a man up with a purpose... to determine if he could potentially make a good boyfriend and ultimately a good husband and father.

Now this is where it gets tricky, ladies...although potential can give you some indication of what a man could become in the future, it is not always what he will become. Sometimes what is perceived to be a guy's potential can be misleading and a setup when a woman begins to set her expectation too high for a guy she thinks she wants. For example, I've heard women say, "He is okay... I guess... but I need (the key word being NEED) him to be more like this or that." Instead of accepting a man for who he is, a woman starts to see him for what she thinks he should be or could become.

If a man does not fulfill or live up to what the woman thinks his potential is, the drama begins. This is when a woman begins to try to mold and shape a man by relentlessly pressuring him into what she wants him to be (men are not experiments, ladies). And I don't have to tell you, if this has been your experience, men don't respond well to a woman trying to change or pressure them. This will only create a lot of frustration on the woman's part and put a huge strain on the relationship. Both will begin to resent one another... the woman because the man will continue to resist her attempts to make him into what she thinks he should be and the man will begin to resent his woman for not accepting him for who he is.

That said... looking for a man with potential can be a good thing but should not be the only basis for getting into a relationship. Potential should be used as a basic guide, criteria or prerequisite if you are looking for certain qualities or basic requirements in a man. This is why having standards are important. Standards are based on what a man has to offer currently and not on what you see or think are a guy's potential. If you want or need certain things from a man right off, why settle or defer what may or may not happen? It is also important to know that potential is only as good as the motivation a person puts behind it. In other words, a man might have the room and the capacity to do better only if he is motivated and puts in the effort. The fact is, some people never live up to their potential. So you should really get to know the man you're dealing with well (or as well as you can) before committing to the relationship.

Bottom line is—if you meet a man you think has potential, you have to accept him for who he is and try not to change him into the person you think he should be or could become. You might also need to accept the fact that he is just not the right one for you and it may be time to move on.

But if you do decide that you want to work with a guy who you think has potential... you can only control what you do and try to be the best you can be in the relationship. You also have to be very careful not to use tactics like being controlling, manipulating, berating, criticizing and pressuring a man for not being what you want him to be. This negative approach has never motivated anyone and will only create more drama and stress in the relationship. It may even push you farther apart.

The man needs to be self-motivated and have the desire to want to be more and do more. If you believe a man you are with has potential to be something more than what he is in your opinion and you have his best interest in mind, it is okay to communicate this to him and let him know he has your support. But more importantly you have to make sure that whatever you think he should be or could be is something he wants too, if the relationship is going to work.

Recap: Potential is only as good as the motivation a person puts behind it. In other words, a man might have the room and the capacity to do better only if he is motivated and puts in the effort.

BONUS CHAPTERS

CHAPTER 23

A Real Man

A "real" man is a term that women are all too familiar with. Women use this term when they are upset with a man, comparing a man, or describing the type of man they are looking for. Some common expressions women use are, "If you were a real man..." or "Why don't you act like a real man..." or "I wish I could find a real man." Well, I feel you, ladies. Men have really been slippin' in the relationship department and not handling their business when it comes to treating you the way you deserve to be treated, so I will give you my perspective on what a "real" man should be and hope men will do their part and step up their game... Com' on, fellas.

Now I'm not knocking all men because if this doesn't apply to you, keep doing what you do. But to my other brothas, a "real" man is a gentleman. No, ladies, chivalry isn't dead. Some men just need to be reminded that it is not about being "soft" or a "punk" if you open a door for a lady, pull out her chair, allow her to walk on the inside if you are walking down street, pay for dinner if you invite her out, or bring her a single rose or flowers on the first date. This is what you call "real game!"

Men need to be reminded that calling women B's, hoes and disrespecting or degrading them is not cool and does not make you a "real" man. Remember, fellas... we all came from a woman. Men also need to be reminded that if you want to play the field or be a so-called "playa," you need to strap up and stop making babies all over the place because this is not what a "real" man does.

Yeah women have some responsibility in this too, but, fellas, you should be taking charge in this area and trust that a woman will respect you more if you're protecting yourself and her. Remember, other things besides babies can come from having un-protected sex (i.e., sexually transmitted diseases). And for the men who already have several babies by different women, com' on, brothas. You've got to step up and take care of these kids because that's what a "real" man does. I know breakups are hard and sometimes it is not easy dealing with "baby mama drama," but you've got to remember that it's not the child's fault and you've got to make sure that the child is still well taken care of. This does not just mean taking care of the child financially, but more importantly, you have to spend quality time with your child. A "real" man also does not disrespect his child's mother just because he has found a new woman to take her place.

Keepin' it one hundred, fellas, a "real" man also understands that there is no romance without finance. If you are thirty-five or older, living at home with your mother, and putting your name on the orange juice, stop it, fellas! This is not to say that you have to be ballin' out of control, but you should have a decent job or have completed some educational goals. Com' on, brothas, this is not that hard if you really want it. A "real" man will bring something to the table and not just eat at it!

In the bedroom, fellas, a "real" man knows it's not just about getting in and out, or what you think you might be packing in terms of how well-endowed you are. It's about stimulating a woman's mind, and I don't just mean telling her how fine she looks or all the things you want to do when you get her home. Sure... there ain't nothing wrong with that because you should have good conversation, give her compliments and tell her how much you love or desire her. But you will stimulate her mind more by doing things like taking out the garbage, washing the dishes, cooking a meal or two, making her breakfast in bed, helping with the kids, managing the bills, or going grocery shopping and putting the food away. On occasion, massage her body from head to toe when she comes home from a long day at work.

Yeah it goes both ways fellas, but a "real" man will do these things just because he cares about his lady and understands how precious she is to him. It shouldn't be about only hooking her up if she hooks you up. You've got to be genuine and selfless in what you do, fellas. Surprise her every now and again with something from the heart and be creative. It doesn't always have to be expensive or on special occasions like anniversaries or Valentine's Day. You've got to keep the ladies guessing. You've got to bring the romance back, fellas—walks on the beach, candle-lit dinners and a little R&B or whatever you need to do to set the mood. It shouldn't always be about taking her upstairs and letting it do what it do with no introduction to the lovemaking.

As for my brothas that are living with women and having babies with them, put a ring on it, fellas. That's what a "real" man does. You've got to honor that woman. If she is good enough to live with and have babies with, she should be good enough to be your wife. The same goes for men who are in these overly extended relationships (you know who you are). Either make an honest woman out of her or let her go so that she could find a man who will give her what she needs. Ladies, you also have to set the standard and not let a man dictate or do what he wants to do just for the sake of having a man. Trust me, ladies, if you respect yourself, and if you've got a good man, he will respect you and do what he needs to do.

The bottom line is... a "real" man has many facets to him, but it is the character and inner qualities of a "real" man that set him apart from the rest. A "real" man is someone who is strong and confident but is not afraid to show sensitivity and warmth when he needs to. He has pride, but is not too prideful to admit his mistakes. A "real" man is someone who says what he means and means what he says. He will uplift and support his woman and not tear her down. A "real" man will lead by example and not follow the crowd (pull your pants up, fellas). He is able to communicate his thoughts and feelings and is not afraid to listen to what the other person has to say. A "real" man is most of all secure with himself, stands tall, and takes responsibility for his actions. He's not a perfect man, but he is always striving to be a better man!

Don't despair, ladies, because there are "real" men around, you've just got to continue to be patient and don't force it. More importantly, you've got to love yourself, have standards (within reason, of course) and don't just settle because you want a man in your life. Like Johnny Cochran said, "If it doesn't fit, you must acquit." Truth is, ladies, if you think you deserve a "real" man who will love, respect, and treat you the way you need to be treated, that is what you should have.

CHAPTER 24

How to Keep the Lovemaking Hot and Spicy

This chapter is primarily for those who are married or in long-term relationships. If you are married or in a long-term relationship, I'm sure you have been asked the question (usually by someone who is single, no doubt), how you can be with just one person sexually and not get bored?

You may have even asked yourself that question at one time or another. I guess there is something to be said about the newness or excitement of meeting someone for the first time and being with them sexually. But let me tell you, nothing can compare to the excitement and intensity of being with someone you know well, are totally comfortable with, and most importantly someone you love.

If you had a chance to experience both, I'm sure you would agree with me that there is no real comparison between a casual fling and having a sexual relationship while being in love. But I think the real question that many married people or those in long-term relationships want to know is how does a couple sustain that excitement and intensity in a relationship, or better yet, how do you keep the lovemaking hot and spicy? This is especially important when life gets in the way, such as the responsibility of raising kids, work, finances, family drama, and so on. But what I say to this is if two people really love each other, and are IN LOVE with each other, that exciting and intense lovemaking can sustain with a little bit of effort on both parts. Let me illustrate my point...

First off, relationships are like anything else, you have to work at them to maintain them. Sorry people... there is no easy way, but the saying is anything in life that's worth having is definitely worth the effort it takes to get it and maintain it.

I think the key to keeping it hot and spicy in a relationship is not just about the physical aspect of a relationship but starts with appreciating what you have and not taking each other for granted. Trust me, if you don't treat your man or woman right, someone else will, and this is REAL TALK! You have to get back to doing the little things like complimenting each other, telling each other how much you appreciate one another, flirting, doing thoughtful gestures (i.e. special gifts, feet or body massages, writing poems or letters about the person you love, or giving them a card of appreciation). You can also go for walks and have quality talks, really listen to each other, reflect on the good times before the kids and responsibilities, and think about the first time you kissed his or her lips and the anticipation of being with that person sexually for the first time.

Now let's get to the physical aspect of keeping it hot and spicy. One way this can be done is through sexual exploration. I think sexual exploration can be great as long as both people in the relationship respect each other and are comfortable with whatever the sexual act is. The sky is the limit in how freaky you want to get. All it takes is a little imagination and creativity.

I also believe if it's not broken, you don't need to fix it. Just keep doing what you do and do more of it. In other words, if you have great sexual chemistry in your relationship, don't feel like you have to do anything different. And if you have the time, do more of it. However, when you are juggling careers and children, lovemaking sometimes can be put on the back burner... I get it. I think in this case to keep it hot and spicy you have to first remember how off the chain or amazing the sexual chemistry was before the careers, the kids, and the responsibilities.

EVERYTHING starts with the mind, like, ladies, when you wore lingerie for the first time with your man, or, fellas, when you put together that mixed tape, CD, or MP3 for that first night with your woman, or when you both hooked up in the back seat of that jeep or some other vehicle or place.

Second, I think it is very important for couples to make time to date. On occasions, agree to play hooky from work and spend a quality day together while the children are at school. You can start off with a nice breakfast in bed and follow it up with a little after breakfast dessert that's not on the menu. You can also throw in a movie while lying in bed and see how far you get before you find yourselves starring in your own movie.

If you still have a little time before you have to pick up the kids, or on another day if necessary, plan massages together followed by relaxing in a hot tub and let things get heated in more ways than one. And if time is really limited, never sleep on a quickie. You can save the extended uncut version for another day. Sometimes you just want to get in and get out and that's okay as long as you both are cool with it.

You can also plan a date night—get a sitter, dress up, and go out for a night on the town to dinner, a movie, or just somewhere romantic that has soft music and good ambience. These are all preludes to what comes later on. Now, ladies, pull out that lingerie that you have tucked away or surprise your man with some new lingerie that will blow his mind.

Now it's time to get to the business at hand. You can sneak off to a hotel even if you can't stay all night, just a couple of hours will do. And if you both are comfortable with it, you can even try role-playing, renting adult movies, or buying sex toys and oils if this is your thing. You can also be creative and explore different sexual positions that will put the ancient art of Kama Sutra to shame. Finally, let the headboards bang and the cops come knockin' because it's about to go down...

Bottom line is... you have to continue to appreciate each other, date each other, and not forget that you were a couple before the kids and the responsibilities of family. Also, ladies and fellas, you've got to always try to keep it sexy. Just because you have each other does not mean taking each other for granted or not doing the things you need to do to keep it hot and spicy. You have to communicate your wants and needs, be creative, open to explore (if you both feel comfortable with this), and be spontaneous whenever possible. You also can't let yourself go, ladies and fellas. Head scarfs, curlers, and flannel pajamas are cool, ladies, but you got to switch up the game from time to time. And men... you got to be mindful of the beer belly and work in a stomach crunch or two. Remember what you did to get him or her. You need to continue to do these things to keep that person. Being in love and making love can be all that and then some, but you have to put in the work to keep it hot and spicy and maintain it.

CHAPTER 25

What Is True Happiness in a Relationship?

This is a big question that I'm sure we have all pondered or asked ourselves at one time or another. Well, the reality is there is no one size fits all criteria and this concept has a lot of different meanings for different people depending on who you ask. I have heard people say that true happiness in a relationship is caring, sharing, understanding, trust, respect and friendship.

Oh yeah... let's not forget about good sex. I have also heard the saying, "you got to have a J-O-B if you want to be with me," or the saying, "If it don't make dollars it don't make sense." I believe DJ Quick said that... I digress... but some people really believe that things like money equal true happiness in a relationship. I guess essentially we all have to decide for ourselves what true happiness means.

But in my opinion, I think true happiness in a relationship should come from a person's inner qualities rather than the outer or superficial qualities a person might have such money, status, nice looks or other physical attributes. I think a lot times we know what's right or good for us (instinctively or with our hearts), but we let a lot of things get in the way of being truly happy in our relationships. Things I believe we, as society, have been conditioned to believe will bring us happiness. As mentioned earlier, choosing a mate based primarily or solely on their outer qualities should not be the most important criteria if you are looking for true happiness. Now don't get me wrong, realistically speaking, the outer qualities of person are usually what first attracts us to that person because we are naturally drawn to what we see, but these qualities should be viewed as merely icing on the cake or cherry on top as the saying goes and not the main dish.

To further illustrate my point, I want you to imagine a shiny new car with no engine or a beautiful cake on the outside with no filling on the inside or a beautiful book cover with horrible content. I think you get my point. Well these are examples of what it means when you chose a person based on the outer qualities and not what's on the inside. The fact is the outer or superficial qualities are just no substitute for the character of a good man or woman.

I will admit, something can be said about the benefits of choosing someone who is compatible or equally yoked in terms of education, values, interests, and even income status. I mentioned income or finances because this can present huge problems in the relationship if there is inequality—like financial strains and power struggles. I think being somewhat equally matched gives you the best chance of having a successful relationship (although not guaranteed) because of what you might share in common. But again, I think love, marriage, and relationships should go beyond just the surface.

Whatever happened to the days when you met someone you liked because of who they were on the inside, the vibe and chemistry was right, and you went with that? We didn't treat every relationship like a Donald Trump "Ultimate Merger." It wasn't about the bank account or status. It was about the connection. Now I get that in today's society it seems more than ever that things like money, looks, status and power have become the standard and expectations that everyone is measured by. But you have to ask yourself the question—will these things really bring me true happiness in a relationship?

Just a Thought...

Think about those you've seen on television or read about in magazines (celebrities and the like) who have looks, wealth, status, power, etc. A lot of those people do not seem any happier in their relationships than the average person. I would even venture to say that just as many people, if not more, with money, power, etc. are in unhappy relationships as those without. The fact is material things or things that lack substance and are superficial do not guarantee true happiness.

The bottom line is... there is nothing wrong with being attracted to the outer qualities of a person or things that glitter or seem like gold. By no means am I knocking these things, but I am trying to make the point that we have taken these things out of context and to the extreme. We have essentially let these factors overshadow and dictate what's truly important in our lives and in our relationships. In my opinion, we've got to get back to the basics and change our way of thinking. If we are looking for true happiness in our relationships, we have to flip the script on our current values and choose people to be in our lives who make us truly happy. We need to feel good from the inside out instead of the outside in.

From the chapter: Eleven Things You Want to Know When You First Meet a Guy

Other questions you might want to know when you first meet a guy:

- How many previous girlfriends has he had? Were they short-term or long-term relationships? What happened to end the relationships? Were the break-ups mutual, did he break them off, or was it the girl who ended things? If he says it was always the other person, this might be questionable. Does he take responsibility for his part in the breakup or always see it as the other person's fault? This might mean he's too self-absorbed to see beyond his own shortcomings or imperfections. Has he learned from his mistakes or been able or willing to work on own issues and grow as a person. If he was cheated on, is he carrying trust issues with him?
- Does he have any strange fetishes?
- Does he like to always be in control? Obviously this speaks to control issues.
- Does he like public displays of affection (PDAs) or not. You want to see if you are compatible in this way (i.e., you're always wanting him to show you affection in public like holding hands, kissing, hugging, etc. and he is not comfortable with this). It could be a problem.
- Does he have a problem with a woman who makes more money? This might speak to insecurity issues.
- Is there any dream he is pursuing that a relationship would interfere with? Just want to make sure you are working on the same page when it comes to pursuing mutual goals and individual goals. No one wants to have resentment later on or be blamed if goals are derailed because of someone's perceived selfishness.

- What does he look for in a woman? Any preferences (physical or character traits)? Have him list his top five (i.e., certain physical make-up or size, complexion, smart, strong, independent, cater to his needs, etc.) See if you fit any of these. If not, is this a problem?
- How does he deal with conflict or disagreements (i.e., does he like to address issues right away, not at all, or at a later time after things have calmed down)? You want to see whether he is a communicator, shuts down or ignores the problem hoping it will go away or resolve itself.

One last thing, ladies... the concepts I have given in this book are just that until you apply them.

Stay up, ladies!

www.ingramcontent.com/pod-product-compliance
Lightning Source LLC
LaVergne TN
LVHW011201080426
835508LV00007B/543